TEACHER'S PET PUBLICATIONS

LITPLAN TEACHER PACK
for
The Giver
based on the book by
Lois Lowry

Written by
Barbara M. Linde, MA Ed.

© 1997 Teacher's Pet Publications
All Rights Reserved

This **LitPlan** for Lois Lowry's
The Giver
has been brought to you by Teacher's Pet Publications, Inc.

Copyright Teacher's Pet Publications 1997
11504 Hammock Point
Berlin MD 21811

Only the student materials in this unit plan (such as worksheets, study questions, and tests) may be reproduced multiple times for use in the purchaser's classroom.

For any additional copyright questions,
contact Teacher's Pet Publications.

www.tpet.com

TABLE OF CONTENTS - *The Giver*

Introduction	6
Unit Objectives	8
Unit Outline	9
Reading Assignment Sheet	10
Study Questions	13
Quiz/Study Questions (Multiple Choice)	24
Pre-Reading Vocabulary Worksheets	45
Lesson One (Introductory Lesson)	61
Nonfiction Assignment Sheet	68
Oral Reading Evaluation Form	71
Writing Assignment 1	73
Writing Evaluation Form	75
Writing Assignment 2	79
Writing Assignment 3	86
Extra Writing Assignments/Discussion ?s	88
Vocabulary Review Activities	95
Unit Review Activities	97
Unit Tests	105
Unit Resource Materials	139
Vocabulary Resource Materials	155

A FEW NOTES ABOUT THE AUTHOR

LOWRY, LOIS (1937-). Lois Lowry is the author of over twenty juvenile novels, and has contributed stories, articles, and photographs to many leading periodicals. Her literary awards are numerous and extensive. She once said that she gauges her success as a writer by her ability to "help adolescents answer their own questions about life, identity, and human relationships."

Lois Lowry was born on March 20, 1937, in Honolulu, Hawaii. At the time of her birth, Lowry's father, Robert, a career army dentist and officer, was stationed near Pearl Harbor. The family separated with the onset of World War II, and Lowry spent the duration of the war with her mother's family in the Amish country of Pennsylvania. Much later, Lowry's wartime experience inspired her fourth novel, *Autumn Street*. As an author, she has often translated her life into fiction for the purpose of helping others who may have suffered under similar circumstances.

Memories of her childhood, as well as her experiences as a parent, have led Lowry to her most popular character, Anastasia Krupnik, the spunky, rebellious, and irreverent adolescent who stars in a series of books that began in 1979. The broad audience appeal of the first Anastasia book prompted Lowry to write another novel featuring her heroine, "I have the feeling she's going to go on forever--or until I get sick of her, which hasn't happened yet." Subsequent Anastasia titles number nine at the current time.

In 1990- Lowry received her highest honors. She was awarded the Newbery Medal, National Jewish Book Award, and Sidney Taylor Award from the National Jewish Libraries, all for her World War II tale of Nazi-occupied Denmark, *Number the Stars*. In this novel she created suspense and tension without wavering from the viewpoint of Annemarie, a child who shows the true meaning of courage. Based on a factual account, the inspiration for this novel came from the stories told to Lowry by a friend who was herself a child in Copenhagen during the long years of the German occupation. In 1994, she was again awarded the Newbery Medal for *The Giver*.

With so many accomplishments in the field of children's literature to her credit, Lowry reflects on her career in the following manner: "When I write, I draw a great deal from my own past. There is a satisfying sense of continuity, for me, in the realization that my own experiences, fictionalized, touch young readers in subtle and very personal ways." Ms. Lowry divides her time between Boston and New Hampshire.

THE NEWBERY MEDAL

The Newbery Medal is named in honor of John Newbery (1713-1767), a British publisher and bookseller in the 1700s. Newbery is known as the father of children's literature because he was the first to propose publishing books specifically for children. The award is presented each year by the American Library Association to the "author of the most distinguished contribution to American literature for children" published during the preceding year. The award was first given in 1922 and is awarded annually. The winning book receives the Newbery Medal and one or more runners-up are also recognized as honor books.

YEAR	TITLE	AUTHOR
1997	*The View From Saturday*	Elaine L. Konigsburg
1996	*The Midwife's Apprentice*	Karen Cushman
1995	*Walk Two Moons*	Sharon Creech
1994	*The Giver*	Lois Lowry
1993	*Missing May*	Cynthia Rylant
1992	*Shiloh*	Phyllis Reynolds Naylor
1991	*Maniac Magee*	Jerry Spinelli
1990	*Number the Stars*	Lois Lowry
1989	*Joyful Noise: Poems for Two Voices*	Paul Fleischman
1988	*Lincoln: A Photobiography*	Russell Freeman
1987	*The Whipping Boy*	Sid Fleischman
1986	*Sarah, Plain and Tall*	Patricia MacLachlan
1985	*The Hero and the Crown*	Robin McKinley
1984	*Dear Mr. Henshaw*	Beverly Cleary
1983	*Dicey's Song*	Cynthia Voigt
1982	*A Visit To William Blake's Inn*	Nancy Willard
1981	*Jacob Have I Loved*	Katherine Ann Patterson
1980	*A Gathering of Days*	Joan W. Blos
1970	*Sounder*	William H. Armstrong
1960	*Onion John*	Joseph Krumgold
1950	*The Door in the Wall*	Marguerite di Angeli
1940	*Daniel Boone*	James Daugherty
1930	*Hitty, Her First Hundred Years*	Rachel Field
1922	*The Story of Mankind*	Hendrik Willhem

INTRODUCTION

This unit has been designed to develop students' reading, writing, thinking, listening and speaking skills through exercises and activities related to The *Giver* by Lois Lowry. It includes twenty lessons, supported by extra resource materials.

The **introductory lesson** introduces students to one main theme of the novel through a group discussion of different types of communities. Following the introductory activity, students are given an explanation of how the activity relates to the book they are about to read.

The **reading assignments** are approximately twenty pages each; some are a little shorter while others are a little longer. Students have approximately 15 minutes of pre-reading work to do prior to each reading assignment. This pre-reading work involves reviewing the study questions for the assignment and doing some vocabulary work for 8 to 10 vocabulary words they will encounter in their reading.

The **study guide questions** are fact-based questions; students can find the answers to these questions right in the text. These questions come in two formats: short answer or multiple choice. The best use of these materials is probably to use the short answer version of the questions as study guides for students (since answers will be more complete) and to use the multiple choice version for occasional quizzes. If your school has the appropriate machinery, it might be a good idea to make transparencies of your answer keys for the overhead projector.

The **vocabulary work** is intended to enrich students' vocabularies as well as to aid in the students' understanding of the book. Prior to each reading assignment, students will complete a two-part worksheet for approximately 8 to 10 vocabulary words in the upcoming reading assignment. Part I focuses on students' use of general knowledge and contextual clues by giving the sentence in which the word appears in the text. Students are then to write down what they think the words mean based on the words' usage. Part II gives students dictionary definitions of the words and has them match the words to the correct definitions based on the words' contextual usage. Students should then have a thorough understanding of the words when they meet them in the text.

After each reading assignment, students will go back and formulate answers for the study guide questions. Discussion of these questions serves as a **review** of the most important events and ideas presented in the reading assignments.

After students complete extra discussion questions, there is a **vocabulary review** lesson which pulls together all of the separate vocabulary lists for the reading assignments and gives students a review of all of the words they have studied.

Following the reading of the book, two lessons are devoted to the **extra discussion questions/writing assignments**. These questions focus on interpretation, critical analysis, and personal response, employing a variety of thinking skills and adding to the students' understanding of the novel. These questions are done as a **group activity.** Using the information they have acquired so far through individual work and class discussions, students get together to further examine the text and to brainstorm ideas relating to the themes of the novel.

The group activity is followed by a **reports and discussion** session in which the groups share their ideas about the book with the entire class; thus, the whole class gets exposed to many different ideas regarding the themes and events of the book.

There are three **writing assignments** in this unit, each with the purpose of informing, persuading, or having students express personal opinions. The first assignment is to **inform:** students compile a job resume. The second assignment is to **persuade:** students persuade a potential employer to hire them. The third assignment is to express a personal **opinion:** students take a position on whether or not the Community should have all of the memories.

In addition, there is a **nonfiction reading assignment.** Students are required to read a piece of nonfiction related in some way to *The Giver*. After reading their nonfiction pieces, students will fill out a worksheet on which they answer questions regarding facts, interpretation, criticism, and personal opinions. During one class period, students make **oral presentations** about the nonfiction pieces they have read. This not only exposes all students to a wealth of information, it also gives students the opportunity to practice **public speaking.**

The **review lesson** pulls together all of the aspects of the unit. The teacher is given four or five choices of activities or games to use which all serve the same basic function of reviewing all of the information presented in the unit.

The **unit test** comes in two formats: all multiple choice-matching-true false or with a mixture of matching, short answer, and composition. As a convenience, two different tests for each format have been included.

There are additional **support materials** included with this unit. The **unit resource** section includes suggestions for an in-class library, crossword and word search puzzles related to the novel, and extra vocabulary worksheets. There is a list of **bulletin board ideas** which gives the teacher suggestions for bulletin boards to go along with this unit. In addition, there is a list of **extra class activities** the teacher could choose from to enhance the unit or as a substitution for an exercise the teacher might feel is inappropriate for his/her class. **Answer keys** are located directly after the **reproducible student materials** throughout the unit The student materials may be reproduced for use in the teacher's classroom without infringement of copyrights. No other portion of this unit may be reproduced without the written consent of Teacher's Pet Publications, Inc.

UNIT OBJECTIVES - *The Giver*

1. Through reading *The Giver,* students will analyze characters and their situations to better understand the themes of the novel.

2. Students will demonstrate their understanding of the text on four levels: factual, interpretive, critical, and personal.

3. Students will practice reading aloud and silently to improve their skills in each area.

4. Students will enrich their vocabularies and improve their understanding of the novel through the vocabulary lessons prepared for use in conjunction with it.

5. Students will answer questions to demonstrate their knowledge and understanding of the main events and characters in *The Giver*.

6. Students will practice writing through a variety of writing assignments.

7. The writing assignments in this are geared to several purposes:
    a. To check the students' reading comprehension
    b. To make students think about the ideas presented by the novel
    c. To make students put those ideas into perspective
    d. To encourage critical and logical thinking
    c. To provide the opportunity to practice good grammar and improve students' use of the English language.

8. Students will read aloud, report, and participate in large and small group discussions to improve their public speaking and personal interaction skills.

UNIT OUTLINE - *The Giver*

1 Introduction	2 PVR 1-2 Study ?s 1-2 Nonfiction Assignment	3 PVR 3-5 Oral Reading Evaluations	4 Mini-Lesson: Setting/Mood Study?s 3-5 PVR 6-7	5 Study ?s 6-7 Writing Assignment #1
6 Mini-Lesson: Plot PVR 8-10	7 Study ?s RA3 PVR 11-14 Quiz 1-10	8 Study ?s 11-13 Writing Assignment #2	9 Writing Conference PVR 14-16	10 Study ?s 14-16 PVR 17-19
11 Study ?s 17-19 PVR 20-23	12 Study ?s 20-23 Mini-Lesson: Character Traits	13 Writing Assignment #3	14 Plot Diagram Extra Discussion ?s	15 Projects
16 Vocabulary Review	17 Unit Review	18 Unit Test	19 Nonfiction Assignment	20 Project Utopia Presentations

Key: P = Preview Study Questions   V = Vocabulary Worksheets   R = Read

READING ASSIGNMENT SHEET - *The Giver*

Date to be Assigned	**Chapters**	**Completion Date** (Prior to Class on This Date)
	Chapters 1-2	
	Chapters 3-5	
	Chapters 6-7	
	Chapters 9-10	
	Chapters 11-13	
	Chapters 14-16	
	Chapters 17-19	
	Chapters 20-23	

STUDY GUIDE QUESTIONS

SHORT ANSWER STUDY GUIDE QUESTIONS - *The Giver*

Chapters 1-2
1. What did the word "frightened" mean, according to Jonas?
2. What were Jonas and the other children taught to be careful about?
3. How did Jonas decide he felt? What was causing this feeling?
4. What evening ritual did the family perform after dinner?
5. What were the two occasions when release was not punishment?
6. What did Father want to do about the newchild, and why?
7. What fascinated Jonas about his father?
8. Why was the Ceremony of Twelve so important?

Chapters 3-5
1. What was unusual about Jonas and the newchild?
2. Describe the Assignment of Birthmother. What did Lily's parents say about it?
3. What happened to the apple while Jonas was playing with it?
4. Describe the Celebration of Release of Roberto.
5. Did Larissa know exactly where Roberto or anyone else went when they were released?
6. What was Jonas's dream about? What did his mother and father say about it?

Chapters 6-7
1. Describe the jacket that the Fours, Fives, and Sixes wore, and the reason it was designed the way it was. Also describe the jacket the Sevens wore, and what it symbolized.
2. Describe the Ceremony. Tell what happened at the Naming and the other age levels.
3. What Assignment did Asher get?
4. What happened when Jonas's number should have been called? What did Jonas think?

Chapters 8-10
1. What was Jonas's Assignment? Why was it important and unusual?
2. What were the four qualities the Chief Elder said the Receiver of Memory must have?
3. What happened when Jonas was looking out at the crowd?
4. Did Jonas agree or disagree with the committee's choice of him as the new Receiver?
5. What happened the last time a new Receiver had been chosen?
6. From what rules was Jonas exempted?
7. What was Jonas prohibited from doing?
8. What was he allowed to do that he had not been allowed to do before?
9. What was the biggest difference in the Receiver of Memory's dwelling?
10. What memories did the Receiver of Memory say he had to transmit to Jonas?
11. What was the first memory the Receiver said he would give to Jonas?

Short Answer Study Guide Questions with Answers *The Giver* page 2

Chapters 11 - 13
1. Describe Jonas's consciousness while he received the memory.
2. What words or concepts did Jonas experience?
3. What happened to the old man's memory of the ride on the sled after he transmitted it to Jonas?
4. What kind of questions did Jonas ask about snow, sleds, and hills? What was the old man's answer? What was Jonas's response?
5. Jonas thought the Receiver of Memory had power. What did the old man tell him?
6. What did the old man tell Jonas to call him? Why?
7. Describe Jonas's experiences of "seeing beyond."
8. What was happening when Jonas "saw beyond?" Why was it important?
9. Could the other people in the Community see colors? If not, why not?
10. Summarize the conversation between Jonas and The Giver about choices.
11. The Giver explained why the people needed a Receiver of Memory. What were the reasons?

Chapters 14-16
1. Jonas asked what made The Giver suffer. What memory did The Giver transmit to explain it?
2. What did Jonas realize about his family after his session with The Giver?
3. Jonas asked why he and The Giver had to hold the memories. What was The Giver's answer? What was his example?
4. What did Jonas want to do about the memories and the traditional way of doing things?
5. How did Jonas help Gabriel get to sleep?
6. What pain did The Giver ask Jonas to take in Chapter 15?
7. How did Jonas feel about being the Receiver at the beginning of Chapter 16?
8. Describe The Giver's favorite memory that he gave to Jonas. How did Jonas feel about it?
9. What question did Jonas ask his parents after his session with The Giver? What was their answer? What was his reaction?
10. Jonas did something different the next morning. What was it?

Short Answer Study Guide Questions with Answers *The Giver* page 3

Chapters 17-19
1. Describe Jonas's new level of feelings and what caused them.
2. What was Father's responsibility when twins were born?
3. How did Jonas feel about becoming the new Receiver?
4. What was the name of the Receiver-to-be who was selected ten years before Jonas?
5. What happened to the Receiver-to-be who was selected before Jonas?
6. What happened to the Community after the incident with the Receiver-to-be?
7. Jonas and The Giver discussed the effects to the Community if Jonas would be lost. What did they think would happen?
8. Describe the release of the newchild.
9. What did Jonas realize as he watched the tape of the release?

Chapters 20-23
1. How did Jonas react after he watched the release?
2. What did The Giver tell Jonas he had realized about the memories?
3. Describe The Giver's ideas on changing things.
4. The Giver offered a very special memory to Jonas. What was it, and what was Jonas's response to the offer?
5. Jonas asked The Giver to escape with him. What was The Giver's reply?
6. What did Jonas do instead of the original escape plan, and why?
7. Describe the escape.
8. Describe the changes in the landscape.
9. What was the strongest fear that Jonas had during this part of the journey?
10. How did the story end?

ANSWER KEY: SHORT ANSWER STUDY QUESTIONS - *The Giver*

Chapters 1-2

1. What did the word "frightened" mean, according to Jonas?
    It was a "deep, sickening feeling of something terrible about to happen."

2. What were Jonas and the other children taught to be careful about?
    They were taught to be careful about language.

3. How did Jonas decide he felt? What was causing this feeling?
    He felt apprehensive. His special Ceremony of Twelve would be coming in December.

4. What evening ritual did the family perform after dinner?
    They shared their feelings.

5. What were the two occasions when release was not punishment?
    Release of the elderly and release of a newchild were not punishment.

6. What did Father want to do about the newchild, and why?
    He wanted to bring the newchild home with him for extra nurturing. The child was not progressing and would be released if he did not improve. Father thought the extra attention would be helpful.

7. What fascinated Jonas about his father?
    His father had broken the rule about looking at the year's Naming list.

8. Why was the Ceremony of Twelve so important?
    The Twelves would get their adult job Assignments. It marked the end of their childhood and preparation for adult life.

Chapters 3-5

1. What was unusual about Jonas and the newchild?
    They both had pale eyes. Most of the Community members had dark eyes.

2. Describe the Assignment of Birthmother. What did Lily's parents say about the it?
    The Birthmothers had three children. They were not allowed to see the children. After the third child, the Birthmothers were given jobs as Laborers for the rest of their lives. The Assignment did not have much honor.

3. What happened to the apple while Jonas was playing with it?
   The apple changed for an instant. Jonas was not sure what the change was, but he knew it had changed.

4. Describe the celebration of Release of Roberto.
   First, he told about his life. Then the attendants toasted, cheered, and chanted the anthem. Then Roberto made a good-bye speech. After that, he bowed and walked through a special door in the Releasing Room.

5. Did Larissa know exactly where Roberto or anyone else went when they were released?
   No, she did not.

6. What was Jonas's dream about? What did his mother and father say about it?
   He had a dream that he wanted Fiona to take off her clothes and get in a bathtub. His parents said it was the Stirrings. His mother gave him a pill that would stop them. She told him he would have to take one every day until he entered the House of the Old.

Chapters 6-7

1. Describe the jacket that the Fours, Fives, and Sixes wore and the reason it was designed the way it was. Also describe the jacket the Sevens wore and what it symbolized.
   The jacket the Fours, Fives, and Sixes wore buttoned down the back so the children would have to help each other dress and learn interdependence. The jacket the Sevens wore had buttons in the front, which symbolized independence and growing up.

2. Describe the Ceremony. Tell what happened at the Naming and the other age levels.
   During the Naming, the Nurturers brought the newchildren to the stage. They received their names and parents. The Eights received new jackets with smaller buttons and pockets. The pockets symbolized maturity and the ability of the wearer to keep track of small possessions. The Nines got their bicycles. The Tens had their long hair cut off. The female Elevens got new undergarments. The male Elevens got longer trousers with a special pocket for their school calculator.

3. What Assignment did Asher get?
   He was named Assistant Director of Recreation.

4. What happened when Jonas's number should have been called? What did Jonas think?
: The Chief Elder skipped Jonas's number. He thought he had done something wrong.

Chapters 8-10

1. What was Jonas's Assignment? Why was it important and unusual?
: Jonas was selected to become the new Receiver of Memory for the Community. It was unusual because the Community only had one Receiver, and he chose his successor. Receiver was the most important job in the Community.

2. What were the four qualities the Chief Elder said the Receiver of Memory must have?
: They were intelligence, integrity, courage, and wisdom.

3. What happened when Jonas was looking out at the crowd?
: They changed, the way the apple had changed.

4. Did Jonas agree or disagree with the committee's choice of him as the new Receiver?
: He agreed with it.

5. What happened the last time a new Receiver had been chosen?
: The girl was not successful. No one really knew exactly what had happened.

6. From what rules was Jonas exempted?
: He was exempted from rules governing rudeness. He could ask anyone any question and he would receive an answer.

7. What was Jonas prohibited from doing?
: He was not allowed to tell his dreams.

8. What was he allowed to do that he had not been allowed to do before?
: He was allowed to lie.

9. What was the biggest difference in the Receiver of Memory's dwelling?
: It was the books. Ordinary people did not have any.

10. What memories did the Receiver of Memory say he had to transmit to Jonas?
: It was the memories of the whole world.

11. What was the first memory the Receiver said he would give to Jonas?
: He said it was the memory of snow.

Chapters 11-13

1. Describe Jonas's consciousness while he received the memory.
    One part of his consciousness knew he was lying on the bed in the Annex room, but another part could experience the sensation of snow and the sled. He could see, even though his eyes were closed.

2. What words or concepts did Jonas experience?
    He experienced *snow, sled, hill, runners,* and *frigid air*.

3. What happened to the old man's memory of the ride on the sled after he transmitted it to Jonas?
    He did not remember it anymore. He had given the memory completely to Jonas.

4. What kind of questions did Jonas ask about snow, sleds, and hills? What was the old man's answer? What was Jonas's response?
    Jonas asked why they did not have the things. The old man said that they had disappeared when the communities got Climate Control. Jonas said he wished they still had snow and the other things.

5. Jonas thought the Receiver of Memory had power. What did the old man tell him?
    The old man said he had honor, but not power, and they were not the same.

6. What did the old man tell Jonas to call him? Why?
    The old man told Jonas to call him The Giver. Jonas was the new Receiver.

7. Describe Jonas's experiences of "seeing beyond."
    It was a short, indescribable change. First it happened with the apple. Next, it happened with the audience at the Auditorium. Then it happened with Fiona. Her hair changed in a way he could not describe.

8. What was happening when Jonas "saw beyond?" Why was it important?
    He was seeing the color red. It was the beginning of his ability to see colors.

9. Could the other people in the Community see colors? If not, why not?
    No, they could not. They gave up that ability when they went to Sameness.

10. Summarize the conversation between Jonas and The Giver about choices.
    Jonas wanted to have colors all the time. He wanted to be able to make decisions, to choose what color to wear. He thought being able to see colors might help Gabriel develop. The Giver said that if people were able to make their own choices, they might choose wrongly. Jonas agreed that it was not safe for people to make choices.

11. The Giver explained why the people needed a Receiver of Memory. What were the reasons?
    They sometimes needed the Receiver to use his memories to help them make decisions. Most of the time, they needed the Receiver to keep all of the old memories so they would not have to have them.

Chapters 14-16

1. Jonas asked what made The Giver suffer. What memory did The Giver transmit to explain it?
   The Giver transmitted a memory of a sledding accident. Jonas fell off the sled and broke his leg.

2. What did Jonas realize about his family after his session with The Giver?
   He realized his family members had never known pain.

3. Jonas asked why he and The Giver had to hold the memories. What was The Giver's answer? What was his example?
   He said the memories gave them wisdom. He explained the request from the Committee of Elders when they wanted to increase the birth rate. The Giver remembered hunger and famine and warfare and told them not to increase the birthrate.

4. What did Jonas want to do about the memories and the traditional way of doing things?
   He wanted to change the traditional way of doing things and give everyone the memories.

5. How did Jonas help Gabriel get to sleep?
   Jonas gave Gabriel a memory of sailing on a lake.

6. What pain did The Giver ask Jonas to take in Chapter 15?
   The Giver transmitted the pain of being injured in a battle during a war.

7. How did Jonas feel about being the Receiver at the beginning of Chapter 16?
   He didn't want to be the Receiver. He wanted his childhood and his friends.

8. Describe The Giver's favorite memory that he gave to Jonas. How did Jonas feel about it?

> There was a tree with lights on it inside a house. Children were unwrapping packages. Jonas perceived family. The Giver explained what Grandparents were. He also gave Jonas the word "love." Jonas liked the memory. He wished his life could be that way although he thought it might be a little bit dangerous.

9. What question did Jonas ask his parents after his session with The Giver? What was their answer? What was his reaction?

> He asked if they loved him. They told him to use more precise language. They said he had used an old, meaningless word. They asked if he understood why it was inappropriate. He lied for the first time and said he did.

10. Jonas did something different the next morning. What was it?

> He did not take his pill.

Chapters 17-19

1. Describe Jonas's new level of feelings, and what caused them.

> He had not taken the pills for the Stirrings for four weeks, and he knew this accounted for some of his feelings. Also, he had the memories from The Giver. He knew much more about Elsewhere than anyone else in the Community.

2. What was Father's responsibility when twins were born?

> He weighed the two, gave the larger to a Nurturer, and cleaned up the smaller one. Then he performed a Ceremony of Release.

3. How did Jonas feel about becoming the new Receiver?

> He was not looking forward to it. He was beginning to understand that he would probably have a difficult and lonely life.

4. What was the name of the Receiver-to-be who was selected ten years before Jonas?

> It was Rosemary.

5. What happened to the Receiver-to-be who was selected before Jonas?

> After five weeks, The Giver transferred loneliness and loss to her. He continued to give her both pleasant and unpleasant memories although he did not give her physical pain. After a while, she went to the Chief Elder and asked to be released. The Elder granted her request.

6. What happened to the Community after the incident with the Receiver-to-be?
   Her memories were released back into the Community. It was very difficult for the members, because they had never experienced the feelings before.

7. Jonas and The Giver discussed the effects to the Community if Jonas would be lost. What did they think would happen?
   The Giver said they would have all of the memories Jonas had received over the year. Jonas said they would not like it. The Giver said he could probably help any of the Community members the way he was helping Jonas. He said he would have to think about it some more.

8. Describe the release of the newchild.
   Father weighed both of the newchildren. He gave the heavier one to the Nurturer. He filled a syringe with a clear liquid, then injected the smaller newchild with it. He was talking cheerfully to the newchild during the procedure. The newchild moved around for a few minutes, then stopped. Then his father put the body in a carton and put the carton in a chute in the wall.

9. What did Jonas realize as he watched the tape of the release?
   From his memories of the war, Jonas recognized that the newchild was dead. He realized his father had killed it.

Chapters 20-23

1. How did Jonas react after he watched the release?
   He cried and became sarcastic.

2. What did The Giver tell Jonas he had realized about the memories?
   He said he realized that memories needed to be shared. His job was lonely because he had to keep all of the memories to himself. He said he was thinking of a plan to change things.

3. Describe The Giver's ideas on changing things.
   The Giver said if Jonas escaped and went Elsewhere, the Community would have to take the memories. He knew it would be hard, but he thought it was possible. He would stay with them to help them, but Jonas could never return.

4. The Giver offered a very special memory to Jonas. What was it, and what was Jonas's response to the offer?
   The Giver offered him music. Jonas said he wanted The Giver to keep it for himself, to have when Jonas was gone.

5. Jonas asked The Giver to escape with him. What was The Giver's reply?
   He said his job was to help the Community become whole. Then he wanted to be with his daughter, Rosemary.

6. What did Jonas do instead of the original escape plan, and why?
   Jonas learned that Gabe was to be released. He escaped that night with Gabe.

7. Describe the escape.
   Jonas took Gabe on his bicycle. They rode all night, then rested during the day. Jonas transmitted calming memories to put Gabe to sleep. They traveled that way for several days. Jonas hid them when the search planes flew overhead. He transmitted memories of cold and snow so the heat-seeking devices could not find them. Finally, the planes stopped searching.

8. Describe the changes in the landscape.
   There were more trees and streams. The forests were thick and dark. They saw their first birds.

9. What was the strongest fear that Jonas had during this part of the journey?
   He was afraid they would starve.

10. How did the story end?
    It began snowing and the ground became hilly. Jonas was forced to leave the bicycle and walk up the hill. When he reached the top, he was flooded with memories of joy. He found a sled at the top of the hill and used it to sled down the hill. On the way down he heard music and people singing.

MULTIPLE CHOICE QUIZ/STUDY QUESTIONS - *The Giver*

Chapters 1-2

1. What word meant a "deep, sickening feeling of something terrible about to happen," according to Jonas?
   - A. premonition
   - B. trembling
   - C. frightened
   - D. release

2. What were Jonas and the other children taught to be careful about?
   - A. They were taught to be careful about language.
   - B. They were taught to be careful about not overeating.
   - C. They were taught to be careful about being respectful to teachers.
   - D. They were taught to be careful about not riding their bikes on the grass.

3. How did Jonas decide he felt?
   - A. He felt irritated.
   - B. He felt fascinated.
   - C. He felt intimidated.
   - D. He felt apprehensive.

4. What was causing this feeling?
   - A. His special Ceremony of Twelve would be coming in December.
   - B. He was failing two subjects in school.
   - C. Some other boys were beating him up, and he was afraid to tell on them.
   - D. He was thinking about a movie he had seen recently.

5. What evening ritual did the family perform after dinner?
   - A. They went for a walk.
   - B. They shared their feelings.
   - C. They prayed together.
   - D. They did the dishes and cleaned the house.

6. What were the two occasions when release was not punishment?
   - A. Release of a newchild and release of a sick person were not punishment.
   - B. Release of an orphan and release of the elderly were not punishment.
   - C. Release of the elderly and release of a newchild were not punishment.
   - D. Voluntary release and release of the mentally incompetent were not punishment.

Multiple Choice Quiz/Study Questions *The Giver* page 2

7. True or False: If the newchild did not progress, it would be released.
    A. True
    B. False

8. What fascinated Jonas about his father?
    A. His father was always cheerful.
    B. His father was the youngest person ever to be head of his department.
    C. He realized he did not know his father's age or first name.
    D. His father had broken the rule about looking at the year's Naming list.

9. True or False: The Ceremony of Twelve marked the end of elementary school and entry into high school.
    A. True
    B. False

Multiple Choice Quiz/Study Questions *The Giver* page 3

Chapters 3-5

1. What was unusual about Jonas and the newchild'?
   A. They both had pale eyes.
   B. They both had red hair.
   C. They both cried a lot when they were babies.
   D. They both had the same name.

2. Lily said she might want a certain Assignment, but her parents said it did not have much honor. Which Assignment was it?
   A. Hairdresser
   B. Cook
   C. Laundry Worker
   D. Birthmother

3. What happened to the apple while Jonas was playing with it?
   A. The apple fell apart.
   B. The apple rolled into the river.
   C. The apple changed for an instant.
   D. The apple disappeared.

4. Which event did **not** happen during Roberto's celebration of release?
   A. He told about his life.
   B. He made a good-bye speech.
   C. The attendants toasted, cheered, and chanted the anthem.
   D. The doctor signed Roberto's release papers.

5. True or False: Larissa know exactly where Roberto and everyone else went when they were released?
   A. True
   B. False

6. What was Jonas's dream about?
   A. He wanted Fiona to take off her clothes and get in a bathtub.
   B. He beat up Asher.
   C. He and Fiona got married without permission.
   D. He became the newchild's father.

Multiple Choice Quiz/Study Questions *The Giver* page 4

7. What did his mother and father say and do about it?
    A. They said his imagination was too active and he should study harder.
    B. They said he was evil and had to go and talk to the Elders about a punishment
    C. They said it was the Stirrings. His mother gave him a pill to stop them.
    D. They told him to keep his dreams to himself and never mention them again.

Multiple Choice Quiz/Study Questions *The Giver* page 5

<u>Chapters 6-7</u>   Match the age level and Ceremony gift.

1.	Ones	A.	jacket with smaller buttons and pockets
2.	Fours, Fives, Sixes	B.	name and parents
3.	Sevens	C.	bicycles
4.	Eights	D.	jacket buttoned down the back
5.	Nines	E.	Assignment
6.	Tens	F.	longer trousers with a pocket
7.	female Elevens	G.	jacket buttoned in the front
8.	male Elevens	H.	had long hair cut off
9.	Twelves	I.	new undergarments

<u>Directions: Match the item and what it symbolized.</u>

10.	jacket with smaller buttons, pockets	J.	independence and growing up
11.	bicycles	K.	a more mature style
12.	jacket buttoned down the back	L.	bodily changes
13.	longer trousers with a pocket	M.	moving out into the Community
14.	jacket buttoned in the front	N.	help each other, learn interdependence
15.	had long hair cut off	O.	taking on adult responsibilities
16.	new undergarments	P.	maturity and keeping track of possessions
17.	Assignment	Q.	carrying a calculator in school

Multiple Choice Quiz/Study Questions *The Giver* page 6

18. What Assignment did Asher get?
    A. He was named Language Coordinator.
    B. He was named Sanitation Laborer.
    C. He was named Junior Partner in the Law Office.
    D. He was named Assistant Director of Recreation.

19. True or False: The Chief Elder called Jonas's number, then told him to wait for last to get his Assignment.
    A. True
    B. False

Multiple Choice Quiz/Study Questions *The Giver* page 7

Chapters 8-10

1. What was Jonas's Assignment?
    A. He was given the Assignment of Mediator Among Communities.
    B. He was given the Assignment of Chief Scribe.
    C. He was given the Assignment of new Receiver of Memory for the Community.
    D. He was given the Assignment of Junior Pilot for the Community Air Force.

2. True or False: The Assignment Jonas received was the most important job in the Community.
    A. True
    B. False

3. The Chief Elder said the person in the job Jona would have needed four qualities. Which of the following was **not** one of them?
    A. intelligence
    B. courage
    C. wisdom
    D. agility

4. True or False: Jonas disagreed with the committee's choice of his Assignment?
    A. True
    B. False

5. True or False: The last person who had been chosen for Jonas's Assignment was not successful.
    A. True
    B. False

6. From what rules was Jonas exempted?
    A. He was exempted from rules governing marriage. He could choose his own wife.
    B. He was exempted from rules governing money. He could carry money and spend it whenever and wherever he wanted.
    C. He was exempted from rules governing travel. He could drive and go anywhere he wanted without asking permission.
    D. He was exempted from rules governing rudeness. He could ask anyone any question and he would receive an answer.

Multiple Choice Quiz/Study Questions *The Giver* page 8

7. What was Jonas prohibited from doing?
    A. He was not allowed to tell his dreams.
    B. He was not allowed to live with his family.
    C. He was not allowed to play with his friends.
    D. He was not allowed to eat meat.

8. What was he allowed to do that he had not been allowed to do before?
    A. He was allowed to skip school.
    B. He was allowed to stay up as late as he wanted.
    C. He was allowed to lie.
    D. He was allowed to choose his own hairstyle.

9. Something in the Annex surprised Jonas, because it was something that the ordinary people did not have. What was it?
    A. It was a television set.
    B. It was an automobile.
    C. It was the books.
    D. It was a refrigerator.

10. True or False: In his new Assignment, Jonas would learn to predict the future.
    A. True
    B. False

11. What did Jonas find out about first?
    A. He found out about rain.
    B. He found out about animals.
    C. He found out about war.
    D. He found out about snow.

Multiple Choice Quiz/Study Questions *The Giver* page 9

Chapters 11-13

1. Which of the following is **not** one of the words or concepts Jonas experienced?
   A. snowball
   B. runners
   C. hill
   D. sled

2. True or False: The old man forgot the memory completely after he had given it to Jonas.
   A. True
   B. False

3. Jonas asked why they did not have the things. What was the old man's answer?
   A. He said a Receiver long before him had lost the memory and now he did not know how to get the things.
   B. He said people had become too weak to know how to deal with the things.
   C. He said that they had disappeared when the communities got Climate Control.
   D. He said another Community had stolen them.

4. True or False: Jonas was glad the people no longer had the other things.
   A. True
   B. False

5. True or False: The old man said honor and power were the same.
   A. True
   B. False

6. What did the old man tell Jonas to call him? What was Jonas?
   A. The old man told Jonas to call him the Recorder. Jonas was the Giver.
   B. The old man told Jonas to call him the Memory Giver. Jonas was the Taker.
   C. The old man told Jonas to call him The Giver. Jonas was the Receiver.
   D. The old man told Jonas to call him the Gifted One. Jonas was the Recipient.

7. What was happening when Jonas "saw beyond?" Why was it important?
   A. He was seeing into things. He was beginning to see into the future.
   B. He was beginning to learn to read minds.
   C. He was seeing the color red. It was the beginning of his ability to see colors.
   D. He was learning to analyze situations in a different way.

Multiple Choice Quiz/Study Questions *The Giver* page 10

8. True or False: Everyone over the age of twelve could do what Jonas could?
   A. True
   B. False

9. Jonas wanted to be able to make decisions. What did the old man say?
   A. He said he thought it was a good idea for Jonas but not for the others.
   B. He agreed.
   C. He said people might make the wrong choices.
   D. He said they should only be allowed to make certain choices.

10. True or False: Jonas agreed with the old man's opinion about choices?
    A. True
    B. False

11. True or False: The people needed a Receiver because they could not read and write.
    A. True
    B. False

Multiple Choice Quiz/Study Questions *The Giver* page 11

Chapters 14-16

1. What memory did The Giver transmit to explain suffering?
    A. Jonas's wife and children died.
    B. Jonas went back in time to the time before the Sameness.
    C. Jonas walked in the desert without food or water.
    D. Jonas fell off a sled and broke his leg.

2. What did Jonas realize about his family after his session with The Giver?
    A. He realized his family members had never known pain.
    B. He realized his family members were not really related to him.
    C. He realized his family members would never understand him.
    D. He realized his family members were not important to him anymore.

3. Jonas asked why he and The Giver had to hold the memories. What did The Giver say?
    A. He said no one else was able to remember things.
    B. He said the others were not brave enough to have memories.
    C. He said the memories gave them wisdom.
    D. He said the people would fight over who got the best memories.

4. True or False: Jonas wanted to change tradition, and give everyone the memories.
    A. True
    B. False

5. How did Jonas help Gabriel get to sleep?
    A. Jonas gave Gabriel a memory of sailing on a lake.
    B. Jonas rocked Gabriel to sleep.
    C. Jonas gave Gabriel a sleeping pill.
    D. Jonas sang to Gabriel.

6. What pain did The Giver ask Jonas to take in Chapter 15?
    A. It was the pain of sunburn.
    B. It was the pain of being injured in a battle during a war.
    C. It was the pain of growing old.
    D. It was the pain of dying of starvation.

Multiple Choice Quiz/Study Questions *The Giver* page 12

7. True or False: Jonas was really happy to be Receiver at the beginning of Chapter 16?
   A. True
   B. False

8. What was The Giver's favorite memory that he gave to Jonas?
   A. It was *happiness* and *party.*
   B. It was *friendship, marriage,* and *children.*
   C. It was *trust* and *caring.*
   D. It was *family, Grandparents,* and *love.*

9. What question did Jonas ask his parents after his session with The Giver? What was their answer?
   A. He asked if he were adopted. They did not know what the word meant.
   B. He asked them to tell about their parents and their childhood. They both said they did not remember.
   C. He asked if they loved him. They told him to use more precise language. They said he had used an old, meaningless word.
   D. He asked if he could bring his children to see them in later years. They got angry and said it was against the laws of the Community.

10. What was his reaction to his parents' answer?
    A. He lied for the first time.
    B. He thanked them for their honesty.
    C. He realized he did not want to live with them anymore.
    D. He was sorry he had ever been given the Assignment of Receiver.

11. Jonas did something different the next morning. What was it?
    A. He walked to school instead of riding his bicycle.
    B. He prayed.
    C. He did not take his pill.
    D. He read a book in front of his family members.

Multiple Choice Quiz/Study Questions *The Giver* page 13

Chapters 17-19

1. Jonas had a new level of feelings caused by the memories from The Giver and what else?
   A. He was reading all of The Giver's books.
   B. He had not taken the pills for the Stirrings for four weeks.
   C. He was eating better. The Giver had the best food in the Community.
   D. He was happy because he did not have to go to school anymore.

2. True or False: Father performed a Ceremony of Release on the younger of the twins.
   A. True
   B. False

3. How did Jonas feel about becoming the new Receiver?
   A. He was excited about learning everything.
   B. He was afraid to get more of the unpleasant memories.
   C. He was not looking forward to it. He was beginning to understand that he would probably have a difficult and lonely life.
   D. He was looking forward to getting all of The Giver's memories and then starting a revolution in the Community.

4. What happened to the Receiver-to-be who was selected before Jonas?
   A. She died young of natural causes.
   B. She fell in love with the Receiver from another Community and ran away.
   C. She went to the Chief Elder and asked to be released.
   D. She refused to take the Assignment and was given a job as a Laborer.

5. True or False: The Receiver-to-be's memories were lost forever to the Giver and the Community.
   A. True
   B. False

6. True or False: The Receiver-to-be's name was Rosemary.
   A. True
   B. False

7. Jonas and The Giver discussed the effects to the Community if Jonas would be lost. How did Jonas think they would feel?
   A. Jonas thought they would not like it.
   B. Jonas said they would be glad to get the memories.

Multiple Choice Quiz/Study Questions *The Giver* page 14

8. Which of the following is the missing step in the release of the newchild?
Father weighed both of the newchildren. He gave the heavier one to the Nurturer. He filled a syringe with a clear liquid, then injected the smaller newchild with it. He was talking cheerfully to the newchild during the procedure. The newchild moved around for a few minutes, then stopped. Then his father ____

   A. called another Community and arranged a trade of newchildren.
   B. gave newchild to another worker who would take it Elsewhere.
   C. weighed and measured it again and falsified the records so it was big enough.
   D. put the body in a carton and put the carton in a chute in the wall.

9. What did Jonas realize as he watched the tape of the release?
   A. The newchild was dead, and his father had killed it.
   B. His father was much more compassionate than he had realized.
   C. His father had broken the law.
   D. His father was a weak and frightened man.

Multiple Choice Quiz/Study Questions *The Giver* page 15

Chapters 20-23

1. How did Jonas react after he watched the release?
    A. He cheered for the newchild.
    B. He cried and became sarcastic.
    C. He became sick to his stomach.
    D. He got angry and violent, and started ripping books apart and throwing them.

2. True or False: The Giver told Jonas he had to keep the memories to himself. He said they should never be shared with the people.
    A. True
    B. False

3. What did The Giver think Jonas should do?
    A. He thought Jonas should ask for Release.
    B. He thought Jonas should take over as Receiver and then help the people change.
    C. He was too upset to give Jonas any advice.
    D. He thought Jonas should escape and go Elsewhere.

4. The Giver offered a very special memory to Jonas. What was it?
    A. The Giver offered him contentment.
    B. The Giver offered him all of the memories of the time before Sameness.
    C. The Giver offered him music.
    D. The Giver offered him wealth.

5. True or False: The Giver said he had to stay and help the people. He wouldn't go with Jonas.
    A. True
    B. False

6. Did Jonas follow the original escape plan?
    A. No, he did not.
    B. Yes, he did.

7. How did they escape?
    A. Jonas took Gabe on his bicycle.
    B. Jonas rowed a boat across the river.
    C. The Giver drove them to the edge of the Community, where a helicopter picked them up.
    D. They walked.

Multiple Choice Quiz/Study Questions *The Giver* page 16

8. What was following them?
    A. Bloodhounds followed them.
    B. A group of angry citizens followed them.
    C. Search planes were following them.
    D. Nothing followed them, because The Giver had advised against it.

9. True or False: Jonas transmitted memories of swimming underwater to slow Gabe's breathing and escape detection by the search devices that measured the oxygen content of the area.
    A. True
    B. False

10. Which of the following was **not** one of the changes in the landscape?
    A. They saw their first birds.
    B. There were more trees and streams.
    C. A huge canyon appeared ahead of them.
    D. The forests were thick and dark.

11. What was the strongest fear that Jonas had during this part of the journey?
    A. He was afraid they would be caught.
    B. He was afraid they would starve.
    C. He was afraid Gabe would die of exposure to the weather.
    D. He was afraid that Elsewhere would turn out to be just like his Community.

12. What happened to the weather?
    A. It got very hot.
    B. It started raining.
    C. There was a tornado.
    D. It began snowing.

13. True or False: Jonas was forced to leave the bicycle and walked all the way to the top of the hill.
    A. True
    B. False

14. What memories flooded Jonas as he reached the top of the hill?
    A. He was flooded with memories of sorrow.
    B. He suddenly remembered Christmas Day.
    C. He understood just how the Sameness had originally happened.
    D. He was flooded with memories of joy.

Multiple Choice Quiz/Study Questions *The Giver* page 17

15. True or False: Jonas found skis at the top of the hill and used them to ski down.
    A. True
    B. False

16. What did Jonas hear on the way down?
    A. He heard people calling his and Gabe's names.
    B. He heard laughter.
    C. He heard bells ringing and sirens wailing.
    D. He heard music and people singing.

ANSWER KEY: MULTIPLE CHOICE QUIZ/STUDY QUESTIONS - *The Giver*

Chapters 1-2	Chapters 3-5	Chapters 6-7		Chapters 8-10	Chapters 11-13
1. C	1. A	1. B	11. M	1. C	1. A
2. A	2. D	2. D	12. N	2. A	2. A
3. D	3. C	3. G	13. Q	3. D	3. C
4. A	4. D	4. A	14. J	4. B	4. B
5. B	5. B	5. C	15. K	5. A	5. B
6. C	6. A	6. H	16. L	6. D	6. C
7. A	7. C	7. I	17. O	7. A	7. C
8. D		8. F	18. D	8. C	8. B
9. B		9. E	19. B	9. C	9. C
		10. P		10. B	10. A
				11. D	11. B

Chapters 14-16	Chapters 17-19	Chapters 20-23	
1. D	1. B	1. B	9. B
2. A	2. B	2. B	10. C
3. C	3. C	3. D	11. B
4. A	4. C	4. C	12. D
5. A	5. B	5. A	13. A
6. B	6. A	6. A	14. D
7. B	7. A	7. A	15. B
8. D	8. D	8. C	16. D
9. C	9. A		
10. A			
11. C			

VOCABULARY WORKSHEETS

VOCABULARY WORKSHEET CHAPTERS 1-2 - *The Giver*

Below are the sentences in which the vocabulary words appear in the text. Read the sentences. Use any clues you can find in the sentences combined with your prior knowledge then write what you think the underlined words mean in the spaces provided.

1. IMMEDIATELY, the rasping voice through the speakers had said.

2. Now, thinking about the feeling of fear as he pedaled home along the river path, he remembered that moment of palpable, stomach-sinking terror when the aircraft had streaked above.

3. I guess I just got distraught watching them.

4. Apprehensive, Jonas decided. That's what I am.

5. He's a sweet little male with a lovely disposition.

6. We have him in the extra care section for supplementary nurturing, but the committee's beginning to talk about releasing him.

7. . . . because it occurred to me that it might enhance his nurturing if I could call him by a name.

8. Well, it was clear to me–and my parents later confessed that it had been obvious to them, too–what my aptitude was.

Part II Match the vocabulary words with their dictionary definitions

___ 1. rasping   A. fearful; anxious
___ 2. palpable   B. easily perceived; obvious
___ 3. distraught   C. a harsh, grating sound
___ 4. apprehensive   D. talent
___ 5. disposition   E. personality
___ 6. nurturing   F. improve
___ 7. enhance   G. very upset; agitated
___ 8. aptitude   H. helping to grow or develop

VOCABULARY WORKSHEET CHAPTERS 3-5 - *The Giver*

Below are the sentences in which the vocabulary words appear in the text. Read the sentences. Use any clues you can find in the sentences combined with your prior knowledge then write what you think the underlined words mean in the spaces provided.

1. Lily, he decided, would have to learn that soon, or she would be called in for <u>chastisement</u> because of her insensitive chatter.

2. "I think I'd like that," Lily said <u>petulantly</u>.

3. No one had mentioned it, not even his parents, because the public announcement had been sufficient to produce the appropriate <u>remorse</u>.

4. All of his volunteer hours would be carefully <u>tabulated</u> at the Hall of Open Records.

5. "And of course," she added <u>primly</u>, "all lives are meaningful. I don't mean that they aren't."

6. The details were murky and <u>vague.</u>

7. The details were <u>murky</u> and vague.

Part II: Match the vocabulary words with their dictionary definitions.

___ 1. chastisement   A. in a precise and proper manner
___ 2. petulantly   B. recorded and filed
___ 3. remorse   C. regret
___ 4. tabulated   D. unspecified; indefinite
___ 5. primly   E. punishment
___ 6. murky   F. dark
___ 7. vague   G. in an ill-tempered way

VOCABULARY WORKSHEET CHAPTERS 6-7 - *The Giver*

Below are the sentences in which the vocabulary words appear in the text. Read the sentences. Use any clues you can find in the sentences combined with your prior knowledge then write what you think the underlined words mean in the spaces provided.

1. The little girl nodded and looked down at herself, at the jacket with its row of large buttons that <u>designated</u> her as a Seven.

2. Jonas stowed his bicycle beside Mother's and made his way through the <u>throng</u> to find his group.

3. He had been given an unusual and special <u>reprieve</u> from the committee, and granted an additional year of nurturing before his Naming and Placement.

4. The audience applause, which was enthusiastic at each naming, rose in an <u>exuberant</u> swell when one parental pair, glowing with pride, took a male newchild and heard him named Caleb.

5. He knew that his parents <u>cringed</u> a little, as he did, when Fritz, who lived in the dwelling next door to theirs, received his bike and almost immediately bumped the podium with it.

6. His <u>transgressions</u> were small ones, always: shoes on the wrong feet, schoolwork misplaced, failure to study adequately for a quiz.

7. But each such error reflected negatively on his parents' guidance and <u>infringed</u> on the Community's sense of order and success.

8. The Instructors of Threes were in charge of the <u>acquisition</u> of correct language.

9. Even the applause, though enthusiastic, seemed <u>serene</u> when Fiona was given the important Assignment of Caretaker of the Old.

10. Jonas sat, <u>dazed</u>, as they moved into the Thirties and then the Forties nearing the end.

Vocabulary Worksheet Chapters 6-7 - *The Giver* Page 2

Part II: Match the vocabulary words to their dictionary definitions.

___ 1. designated   A. confused; bewildered
___ 2. throng   B. violations of laws or rules
___ 3. reprieve   C. pardon
___ 4. exuberant   D. purchase
___ 5. cringed   E. high-spirited
___ 6. transgressions   F. indicated; pointed out
___ 7. infringed   G. calm
___ 8. acquisition   H. shrank back in fear
___ 9. serene   I. intruded
___10. dazed   J. crowd

VOCABULARY WORKSHEET CHAPTERS 8-10 - *The Giver*

Below are the sentences in which the vocabulary words appear in the text. Read the sentences. Use any clues you can find in the sentences combined with your prior knowledge then write what you think the underlined words mean in the spaces provided.

1. They applauded at the final Assignment; but the applause was piecemeal, no longer a crescendo of united enthusiasm.

2. The Community, relieved from its discomfort by her benign statement, seemed to breathe more easily.

3. I apologize to you in particular. I caused you anguish.

4. Therefore the selection must be sound. It must be a unanimous choice of the Committee.

5. Then she turned and left the stage, left him there alone, standing and facing the crowd, which began spontaneously the collective murmur of his name.

6. From this moment you are exempted from the rules governing rudeness.

7. From this moment you are prohibited from dream-telling.

8. But the most conspicuous difference was the books.

9. The failure of the previous selection was ten years ago, and my energy is starting to diminish.

10. At first it's exhilarating: the sled; the sharp, clear air; but then the snow accumulates, builds up on the runners, and you slow, you have to push hard to keep going, and. . ."

Vocabulary Worksheet Chapters 8-10 - *The Giver* Page 2

Part II: Match the vocabulary words to their definitions.

____ 1. crescendo   A. decrease
____ 2. benign   B. agonizing physical or mental pain
____ 3. anguish   C. noticeable
____ 4. unanimous   D. freed from obligation
____ 5. spontaneously   E. causing to feel energetic
____ 6. exempted   F. unrehearsed
____ 7. prohibited   G. a gradual increase in volume
____ 8. conspicuous   H. complete agreement
____ 9. diminish   I. harmless
____ 10. exhilarating   J. forbidden

VOCABULARY WORKSHEET CHAPTERS 11-13 - *The Giver*

Below are the sentences in which the vocabulary words appear in the text. Read the sentences. Use any clues you can find in the sentences combined with your prior knowledge then write what you think the underlined words mean in the spaces provided.

1. He was filled with energy, and he breathed again, feeling the sharp intake of <u>frigid</u> air.

2. He could see a bright, whirling <u>torrent</u> of crystals in the air around him, and he could see them gather on the backs of his hands, like cold fur.

3. <u>Tentatively</u> he opened his eyes–not his snow-hill-sled eyes, for they had been open throughout the strange ride.

4. It wasn't a practical thing, so it became <u>obsolete</u> when we went to Sameness.

5. You should be able to <u>perceive</u> the name without being told.

6. He was aware of his own <u>admonition</u> not to discuss his training.

7. When I was observing you, before the selection, I perceived that you probably had the <u>capacity</u>, and what you describe confirms that.

8. it was so–oh, I wish language were more <u>precise</u>.

9. "You've come quickly to that <u>conclusion</u>," he said.

10. "It was <u>chaos</u>," he said.

Vocabulary Worksheet Chapters 11-13 - *The Giver* Page 2

Part II: Match the vocabulary words to their definitions.

    ____ 1. frigid   A. no longer in use
    ____ 2. torrent   B. to become aware of through the senses
    ____ 3. tentatively   C. exact
    ____ 4. obsolete   D. the end or finish
    ____ 5. perceive   E. a heavy downpour
    ____ 6. admonition   F. ability to learn
    ____ 7. capacity   G. uncertain; hesitant
    ____ 8. precise   H. confusion
    ____ 9. conclusion   I. very cold
    ____ 10. chaos   J. a reminder of a forgotten task or duty

VOCABULARY WORKSHEET CHAPTERS 14-16 - *The Giver*

Below are the sentences in which the vocabulary words appear in the text. Read the sentences. Use any clues you can find in the sentences combined with your prior knowledge then write what you think the underlined words mean in the spaces provided.

1. The sled moved forward, and Jonas grinned with delight, looking forward to the breathtaking slide down through the invigorating air.

2. It was not enough to assuage the pain that Jonas was beginning, now, to know.

3. Excruciating hunger and starvation.

4. Now it was ominous. It meant, he knew, that nothing could be changed.

5. Gabriel had been bathed and was lying, for the moment, hugging his hippo placidly in the small crib that had replaced the basket. . . .

6. The Giver looked up at him, his face contorted with suffering.

7. In one ecstatic memory he had ridden a gleaming brown horse across a field that smelled of damp grass, and had dismounted beside a small stream from which both he and the horse drank cold, clear water.

8. The Nurturers were very optimistic about Gabriel's future.

Vocabulary Worksheet Chapters 11-13 - *The Giver* Page 2

Part II: Match the vocabulary words to their definitions.

___ 1. invigorating   A. hopeful; expecting the best
___ 2. assuage   B. twisted; disfigured
___ 3. excruciating   C. unfavorable; threatening
___ 4. ominous   D. to relieve
___ 5. placidly   E. overjoyed
___ 6. contorted   F. peacefully
___ 7. ecstatic   G. agonizing
___ 8. optimistic   H. refreshing; stimulating

VOCABULARY WORKSHEET CHAPTERS 17-19 - *The Giver*

Below are the sentences in which the vocabulary words appear in the text. Read the sentences. Use any clues you can find in the sentences combined with your prior knowledge then write what you think the underlined words mean in the spaces provided.

1. And his new, heightened feelings <u>permeated</u> a greater realm than simply his sleep.

2. Feelings <u>surged</u> within Jonas.

3. "Me," Jonas said in a <u>dejected</u> voice.

4. The Giver looked at him <u>gravely</u>. "You must stay away from the river, my friend," he said.

5. "<u>Wretched</u> with happiness."

Part II: Match the vocabulary words with their definitions.

___ 1. permeated   A. requiring serious thought
___ 2. surged   B. spread or flowed throughout
___ 3. dejected   C. depressed
___ 4. gravely   D. miserable
___ 5. wretched   E. increased suddenly

VOCABULARY WORKSHEET CHAPTERS 20-23 - *The Giver*

Below are the sentences in which the vocabulary words appear in the text. Read the sentences. Use any clues you can find in the sentences combined with your prior knowledge then write what you think the underlined words mean in the spaces provided.

1. It's the same life that you would have, if you had not been chosen as my successor.

2. She's very efficient at her work, your red-haired friend.

3. By midday Jonas's absence would become apparent, and would be a cause for serious concern.

4. All of it–all the things they had thought through so meticulously–fell apart.

5. "Yes, we did," Mother agreed emphatically.

6. Together the fugitives slept through the first dangerous day.

7. As he pedaled through the nights, through isolated landscape now, with the communities far behind and no sign of human habitation around him or ahead, he was constantly vigilant, looking for the next nearest hiding place should the sound of engines come.

8. It was a subtle change, hard to identify at first.

9. During his twelve years in the Community he had never felt such simple moments of exquisite happiness.

10. But the hill was treacherously steep; he was impeded by the snow and his own lack of strength.

Vocabulary Worksheet Chapters 20-23 - *The Giver* Page 2

Part II: Match the vocabulary words to their definitions.

____ 1. successor   A. visible; easily seen
____ 2. efficient   B. people running away
____ 3. apparent   C. lovely
____ 4. meticulously   D. one who comes next
____ 5. emphatically   E. extremely concerned with details
____ 6. fugitives   F. alert; watchful
____ 7. vigilant   G. stopped progress
____ 8. subtle   H. indirect; faint
____ 9. exquisite   I. expressed forcefully
____ 10. impeded   J. done with a minimum of waste

ANSWER KEY: VOCABULARY WORKSHEETS - *The Giver*

Chapters 1-2	Chapters 3-5	Chapters 6-7	Chapters 8-10
1. C	1. E	1. F	1. G
2. B	2. G	2. J	2. I
3. G	3. C	3. C	3. B
4. A	4. B	4. E	4. H
5. E	5. A	5. H	5. F
6. H	6. F	6. B	6. D
7. F	7. D	7. I	7. J
8. D		8. D	8. C
		9. G	9. A
		10. A	10. E

Chapters 11-13	Chapters 14-16	Chapters 17-19	Chapters 20-23
1. I	1. H	1. B	1. D
2. E	2. D	2. E	2. J
3. G	3. G	3. C	3. A
4. A	4. C	4. A	4. E
5. B	5. F	5. D	5. I
6. J	6. B		6. B
7. F	7. E		7. F
8. C	8. A		8. H
9. D			9. C
10. H			10. G

DAILY LESSONS

LESSON ONE

Objectives
    1. To preview *The Giver*
    2. To distribute books and other related materials
    3. To relate prior knowledge to the new material
    4. To discuss different types of communities
    5. To become acquainted with Project Utopia

Activity #1

    Prior to class, gather a supply of magazines with pictures of different types of communities and groups. When class starts, distribute the magazines and have the students look for pictures of communities and groups of people. Ask students to describe their pictures to the class and to describe what they think life in the Community is like. Invite students to discuss their communities, including lifestyle, rules and regulations, family structures, and education. Tell them they will be reading a story about a young boy who lives in a community that is very different from theirs.

Activity #2

    Distribute the materials students will use in this unit. Explain in detail how students are to use these materials.

    Study Guides Students should read the study guide questions for each reading assignment prior to beginning the reading assignment to get a feeling for what events and ideas are important in the section they are about to read. After reading the section, students will (as a class or individually) answer the questions to review the important events and ideas from that section of the book. Students should keep the study guides as study materials for the unit test.

    Vocabulary Prior to reading a reading assignment, students will do vocabulary work related to the section of the book they are about to read. Following the completion of the reading of the book, there will be a vocabulary review of all the words used in the vocabulary assignments. Students should keep their vocabulary work as study materials for the unit test.

Reading Assignment Sheet You need to fill in the reading assignment sheet to let students know by when their reading has to be completed. You can either write the assignment sheet up on a side blackboard or bulletin board and leave it there for students to see each day, or you can "ditto" copies for each student to have. In either case, you should advise students to become very familiar with the reading assignments so they know what is expected of them.

Extra Activities Center The resource sections of this unit contain suggestions for an extra library of related books and articles in your classroom as well as crossword and word search puzzles. Make an extra activities center in your room where you will keep these materials for students to use. (Bring the books and articles in from the library and keep several copies of the puzzles on hand.) Explain to students that these materials are available for students to use when they finish reading assignments or other class work early.

Nonfiction Assignment Sheet Explain to students that they each are to read at least one non-fiction piece related to the ideas presented in *The Giver* at some time during the unit. Students will fill out a nonfiction assignment sheet after completing the reading to help you evaluate their reading experiences and to help the students think about and evaluate their own reading experiences.

Books Each school has its own rules and regulations regarding student use of school books. Advise students of the procedures that are normal for your school.

Activity #3
 Do a group KWL Sheet with the students (form included). Some students will know something about Lois Lowry or her books and will have information to share. Put this information in the K column (What I Know). Ask students what they want to find out from reading the book and record this in the W column (What I Want To Find Out). Keep the sheet and refer back to it after reading the book. Complete the L column (What I Learned) at that time.

Activity #4
 Introduce Project Utopia. Ask for input and ideas from the students.

KWL Sheet - *The Giver*

Before reading, think about what you already know about Lois Lowry and/or *The Giver*. Write the information in the K column. Think about what you would like to find out from reading the book. Write your questions in the W column. After you have read the book, use the L column to write the answers to your questions from the W column, and anything else you learned from the book.

K (What I Know)	W (What I Want to Find Out)	L (What I Learned)

PROJECT UTOPIA

The Project

Project Utopia is a small group project for use in conjunction with the novel, *The Giver*. Since the descriptions of the utopian community life are so central to the understanding of the novel, this will be a good opportunity for the students to explore different kinds of communities. You, the teacher, should be able to meet some English/Language Arts and Social Studies learning objectives by having students complete the project.

This project is separate from the rest of the unit on *The Giver*. Having it as a separate project allows for more flexibility without interrupting the normal flow of the unit. It can be used either while students are reading *The Giver*, it can be used as a separate mini-unit after the book has been read, or it can be eliminated if necessary.

Objectives

1. Students will work cooperatively in a small group.
2. Students will develop research skills by using reference books, interviews, on-line databases, and other information sources.
3. Students will write a description and explanation of their model community.

Forming Work Groups

Either assign students to groups of 4 to 6 or allow them to choose their own group members. Then have the group choose a coordinator and a recorder. Other tasks can be discussed on an as-needed basis.

Assignment #1

Discuss the concept of a utopian community. (An ideal place or state with perfect laws.) Students should spend some time researching different types of communities (past, present, and future). Encyclopedias, television documentaries, and online sources can be used. A variety of literary genre, such as science fiction, fiction, and historical fiction may also be used. (NOTE to the teacher: You may want to use this research to fulfill the students' nonfiction reading assignment.)

Assignment #2

Have student groups discuss different types of communities. Then have them decide on the kind of community they would like to create. The community should include the following:

" Community's name
" Size of the community
" Roles and responsibilities of community members
" Education and religion
" Government type and structure
" Location and physical description
" Laws and punishments
" Delivery of goods and services

Project Utopia Page 2

Assignment #3

Have each group prepare a written report describing its community. A suggested length for the report is one page per topic. Assign whatever length is appropriate for the level of your students.

Assignment #4

Tell each group to make a poster outlining the key facts about their community. They can also make a diorama or other model of the community for extra credit.

Assignment #5

Invite each group to give a 10-20 minute oral report to the class. Groups may choose one spokesperson or have all group members participate. Encourage students to dress and speak as the members of the community would.

Grading

Grading criteria is the decision of the individual teacher.

LESSON TWO

Objectives
1. To become familiar with the vocabulary for Chapters 1-2
2. To preview the study questions for Chapters 1-2
3. To read Chapters 1-2
4. To make predictions
5. To discuss the main ideas and themes in Chapters 1-2
6. To become familiar with the Nonfiction Assignment

Activity #1

Work through the pre-reading vocabulary worksheet for Chapters 1-2 with the students. Tell them they will have a sheet like this to complete before reading each section of the book.

Activity #2

Show students how to preview the study questions for Chapters 1-2 of *The Giver*. Encourage students to predict what they think answers might be and to compare their predictions with their answers after reading the chapters.

Activity #3

Ask students to speculate on who The Giver in the title is and what he/she may be giving. You may want to read Chapter 1 aloud to the students to set the mood for the novel. Invite willing students to read Chapter 2 aloud to the class.

Activity #4

Discuss the concept of "release." Ask students to predict what happens when someone is released from the Community.

Activity #5

Discuss the answers to the Study Guide questions for Chapters 1 and 2 in detail. Write the answers on the board or use the overhead projector so students can have the correct answers for study purposes. Encourage students to take notes. If the students own their own books, encourage them to use highlighter pens to mark important passages and the answers to the study questions.

NOTE: It is a good practice in public speaking and leadership skills for individual students to take charge of leading the discussion of the study questions. Perhaps a different student could go to the front of the class and lead the discussion each day that the study questions are discussed during this unit. Of course, the teacher should guide the discussion when appropriate and be sure to fill in any gaps the students leave.

Activity #6
    Distribute copies of the Nonfiction Assignment Sheet and go over it in detail with the students. Explain to students that they are to read at least one nonfiction piece at some time during the unit. This could be a book, a magazine article, or information from an encyclopedia or from the Internet. Students will fill out a nonfiction assignment sheet after completing the reading to help you (the teacher) evaluate their reading experiences and to help themselves think about and evaluate their own reading experiences. Give them the due date for the assignment (Lesson 18).
    Encourage students to read about topics that are related to the theme of the novel. They may want to tie this assignment to their research for Project Utopia. Some suggestions are: types of governments, social, community, and family structures (such as the Shakers, Quakers, Amish, Mennonites, a Native American tribe, or a Hasidic Jewish community), the roles of children, adults, or the elderly in society, different types of jobs and occupations, the way people cope with emotions and feelings, euthanasia, diversity, language precision/word meanings, speech styles from other eras or cultures, the nature of color, or the way the eye and brain perceive color.

NONFICTION ASSIGNMENT SHEET - *The Giver*
(To be completed after reading the required nonfiction article)

Name _____ Date _____

Title of Nonfiction Read _____

Written By _____ Publication Date _____

I. Factual Summary: Write a short summary of the piece you read.

II. Vocabulary
    1. With which vocabulary words in the piece did you encounter some degree of difficulty?

    2. How did you resolve your lack of understanding with these words?

III. Interpretation: What was the main point the author wanted you to get from reading his work?

IV. Criticism
    1. With which points of the piece did you agree or find easy to accept? Why?

    2. With which points of the piece did you disagree or find difficult to believe? Why?

V. Personal Response: What do you think about this piece? OR How does this piece influence your ideas?

LESSON THREE

Objectives
1. To become familiar with the vocabulary for Chapters 3-5
2. To preview the study questions for Chapters 3-4
3. To read Chapters 3-5 orally for evaluation
4. To practice correct intonation and expression in oral reading

Activity #1
   Give students about fifteen minutes to preview the study questions for Chapters 3-5 and do the related vocabulary work.

Activity #2
   Tell students their oral reading ability will be evaluated. Show them copies of the Oral Reading Evaluation Form and discuss it. Model correct intonation and expression by reading the first few paragraphs for Chapter 3 aloud.

Activity #3
   Call on individual students to read a few paragraphs aloud. Encourage the other students to follow along silently in their books. If you have a student who is unwilling or unable to read in front of the group, make arrangements to do his or her evaluation privately at another time.

LESSON FOUR

Objectives
1. To review the main ideas and themes in Chapters 3-5
2. To discuss the setting of the novel
3. To become familiar with the vocabulary for Chapters 6-7
4. To preview the study questions for Chapters 6-7

Activity #1
   Go over the answers to the study guide questions for Chapters 3-5. Encourage students to correct any errors they have.

Activity #2: Mini-Lesson: Setting and Mood

Tell students the setting of a story includes geographical, physical, and historical aspects. It makes the reader familiar with the place and time of the story. Use one of the following activities to help students identify various settings (place and time). Read a short, familiar story such as *Where the Wild Things Are* or *Hansel and Gretel.* Have students listen and look at the pictures, then describe the setting, OR show magazine pictures of various settings. Have students describe them.

Explain that mood refers to the atmosphere or emotional context of the story. The author develops the mood of the story at least partially through the description of the setting. Invite students to look again at the books or pictures used to illustrate the setting. Have them describe the mood they sense.

Tell students to pay particular attention to the mood and setting of *The Giver* as they read Chapters 6-7. After they have read the chapters, discuss the setting and mood. You may want the students to illustrate or cut out pictures that represent the setting and mood of the novel.

NOTE: The only aspects of the setting that are described in detail are the month (almost December and throughout the following year) and the Community. Discuss the impact of this lack of definite setting on the reader. Invite students to speculate on a more exact setting.

ORAL READING EVALUATION - *The Giver*

Name _____ Class____ Date _____

SKILL	EXCELLENT	GOOD	AVERAGE	FAIR	POOR
Fluency	5	4	3	2	1
Clarity	5	4	3	2	1
Audibility	5	4	3	2	1
Pronunciation	5	4	3	2	1
_____	5	4	3	2	1
_____	5	4	3	2	1

Total _____ Grade _____

Comments:

LESSON FIVE

Objectives
1. To review the main events and ideas in Chapters 6-7
2. To practice writing to inform

Activity #1
Invite students to work in small groups to either dramatize or illustrate the answer to one of the study guide questions. Allow time for each group to present its answer.

Activity #2
Discuss the practice in *The Giver* of the Elders' assigning jobs to the Twelves. Ask students what they think their Assignments would be. Then discuss the kinds of occupations and careers the students think they would really like to have. Tell students they will be preparing a resume for that job.

Activity #3
Distribute copies of Writing Assignment #1. Go over the assignment in detail with the students. Tell them they will have the remainder of the class period to begin working on the assignment. Give the due date for the completed assignment.

Activity #4
Distribute copies of the Writing Evaluation Form (included with this guide). Explain to students that during Lesson Nine you will be holding individual writing conferences about this assignment. Make sure students are familiar with the criteria on the Writing Evaluation Form.

NOTE: You may want students to prepare their final drafts of their compositions on a computer or word processor. Display the final copies on a bulletin board.

Follow-Up
After you have graded the assignments, have a writing conference with each student. This guide schedules one in Lesson Nine. After the writing conference, allow students to revise their papers using your suggestions to complete the revisions. Grade the revisions on an A-C-E scale: A=all revisions well done; C=some revisions made; E=few or no revisions made. This will speed your grading time and still give some credit for the students' efforts.

WRITING ASSIGNMENT #1 - *The Giver*

PROMPT
You are applying for a job. The first thing you need to do is write a resume. A resume is a brief summary of your qualifications and work experiences. If you have never seen a resume, ask someone who has one to show it to you. There are books in the library that have sample resumes. A sample resume is also provided here for you. NOTE: The information on the sample resume is only provided as an outline for the kind of information you should include. It is purely a work of fiction. It does not reflect the actual experiences that are necessary to becoming a lifeguard.

PRE-WRITING
The resume should have several parts. In the first part, list your personal information (name, address, telephone number). Next, write a one or two sentence summary about the job you desire. In the next section, list your educational experiences. You may want to include your grade point average, but it is not required. Next briefly describe your three or four best skills or talents. Then list any work experience that you have had. Include volunteer experiences. Tell a little bit about the kinds of responsibilities you had and what your achievements were. Next list any clubs or organizations to which you belong. You may include a section describing your interests and hobbies, especially if they are related to the job you want. You may include church or other community related activities. You do not have to mention your religion if you don't want to. Before you start writing, you need to gather all of the necessary information. Make sure that the names, addresses, and other information are correct.

DRAFTING
A resume is different from an expository paper. You will not write in paragraphs but rather in a modified list form.

When you list your education and work experiences, start with your most recent ones and work backwards. Your earliest school and first job should be the last ones in those sections.

In almost all cases, the resume should be no more than one page long.

PEER CONFERENCING/REVISING
When you finish the rough draft of your resume, ask another student to look at it. After reading your rough draft, he/she will tell you what he/she liked best about your work, which parts were not clear, and ways in which your work could be improved. Reread your resume considering your critic's comments and make the corrections you think are necessary.

PROOFREADING/EDITING
Do a final proofreading of your resume, double-checking your grammar, spelling, organization, and the clarity of your ideas.

FINAL DRAFT
Follow your teacher's guidelines for the final draft of your resume.

Sample Resume

Your Name
Your Address
Your Telephone Number (including area code)

Career Objectives
    Lifeguard/Swimming Instructor

Education
    Central High School, City, State, Current Year
    Oak Street Middle School, City, State, Years There (1996-1998, for example)
    Main Street Elementary School, City, State, Years There

Primary Skills
    Earned Water Safety Certificate, Scout Program, 1998
    Certified Red Cross Lifeguard, 1996
    Passed Red Cross Babysitting Class, 1995

Work Experience
    Lifeguard, York City Pool, Summers 1998 and 1997
    Babysitting for families with from one to six children since 1995
    Volunteer lifeguard/childcare for various church activities, 1996-present

Memberships/Activities
    Church Youth Group, 1998-present. President, 1999
    National Honor Society
    American Red Cross
    Boy Scouts of America 1991-present
    School Soccer Team
    Odyssey of the Mind 1996-1998

References are available upon request.

WRITING EVALUATION FORM - *The Giver*

Name _____ Date _____

       Grade _____

Circle One For Each Item:

Grammar: correct   errors noted on paper

Spelling: correct   errors noted on paper

Punctuation: correct   errors noted on paper

Legibility: excellent   good   fair   poor

Strengths:

Weaknesses:

Comments/Suggestions:

LESSON SIX

Objectives
1. To understand plot development and record plot information on a chart
2. To become familiar with the vocabulary for Chapters 8-10
3. To preview the study questions for Chapters 8-10
4. To read Chapters 8-10 aloud with a partner

Activity #1 Mini-Lesson: Plot

Tell students they will be discussing and mapping the plot of the novel. PLOT refers to the events in the novel. It tells what the characters do, what happens to them, and how things happen. Physical and mental/emotional occurrences are included. The plot is usually told in sequence although flashbacks may be included. Plot structure is usually either conflict-resolution or goal-achievement oriented. The main types of conflicts are character vs. character, character vs. nature, character vs. self, and character vs. society. The CLIMAX is the highest point of action or suspense. The reader does not yet know the outcome. The RESOLUTION or OUTCOME occurs near the end of the story. Some stories may have multiple conflicts or a combination of conflict-resolution and goal-achievement.

Use the Plot Diagram to help students identify the main conflicts and events in the novel. Go over the format before reading and encourage students to identify conflicts as they read. Remind them that they may have to make inferences before drawing their conclusions. After reading Chapters 8-10, compare the beginning of the plot diagram with students.

Discuss the conflicts that have occurred in the story so far and the characters' reactions to them. Have students add the information to their diagrams. Remind students that the climax is the most intense or deeply felt point of the story. The reader will respond to it emotionally. The climax follows some type of crisis in the plot and involves a turning point in the action of the story. Suggest that they keep this information in mind as they read the rest of the novel and look for the climax. Tell them they will complete the plot diagram during Lesson Thirteen.

Activity #2

Give students about fifteen minutes to go over the study guide questions and do the pre-reading vocabulary worksheets.

Activity #3

Have students read Chapters 8-10 aloud and fill in the plot diagram as they read.

Activity #4

Tell students they will be having a quiz on Chapters 1-10 during the next class period.

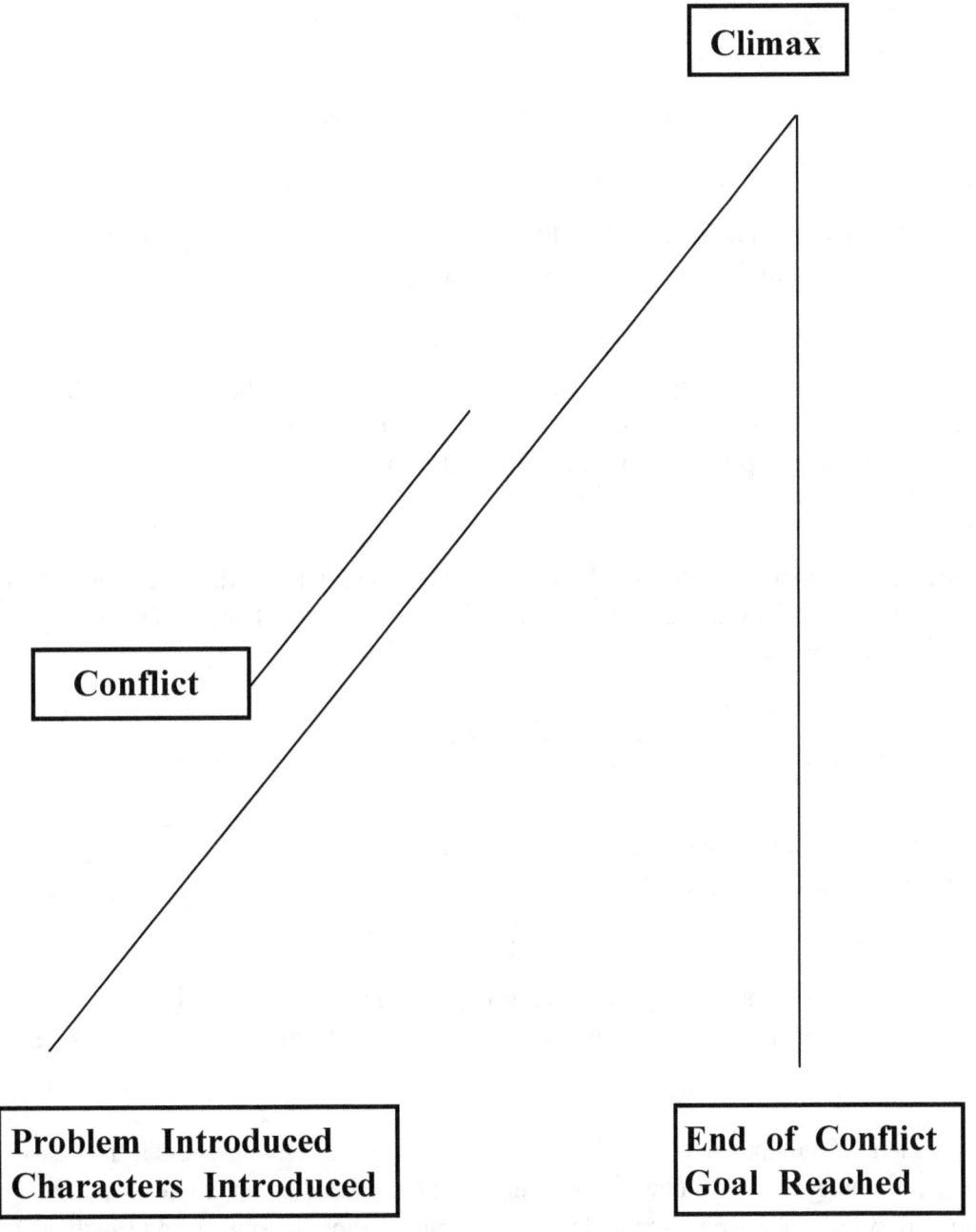

LESSON SEVEN

Objectives
1. To review the main events and ideas in Chapters 8-10
2. To check students' understanding of the main ideas and events in Chapters 1-10
3. To become familiar with the vocabulary for Chapters 11-13
4. To preview the study questions for Chapters 11-13
5. To read Chapters 11-13

Activity #1

Go over the answers to the study questions for Chapters 8-10.

Activity #2

Distribute quizzes (multiple choice study questions from Chapters 1-10) and give students ample time to complete them. Collect the papers for grading.

Activity #3

Before having students complete the vocabulary worksheet for Chapters 11-13, list the words on the board. Invite students to tell what they think the words mean. Then have the students complete the worksheet. They can compare their guesses to the actual meanings of the words.

Activity #4

Have students either read Chapters 11-13 silently or aloud quietly with a partner. If they finish reading early, they can work on the answers to the study questions. Tell them to have the answers completed before the next class meeting.

LESSON EIGHT

Objectives
1. To discuss the main ideas and events in Chapters 11-13
2. To practice writing to persuade

Activity #1

Tell students to work in small groups and discuss the answers to the study guide questions for chapters 11-13. Circulate among the groups and add information to students' answers as necessary.

Activity #2

Ask students if they have ever applied for jobs and to describe the process if they have. Tell them in their next writing assignment they will develop a letter persuading an employer to hire them. NOTE: You may want to allow time for students to role play the job interviews and use the persuasive speeches they have prepared.

WRITING ASSIGNMENT #2 - *The Giver*

PROMPT

You have completed your resume (Writing Assignment #1) and have an interview with the personnel department scheduled for next week. In the interview, you need to persuade the employer that you are the best person for the job. One way to prepare for an interview is to write all of your thoughts down on paper first.

PRE-WRITING

Make sure you know what the employers' needs are, who the clients are, and what the business or service provided is like. Then decide what kinds of things the employer needs to know about you and how you would be an asset to the company. Think of every possible reason the person might hesitate to hire you and think of a counter-argument stating why he/she *should* hire you.

DRAFTING

Write out the list of possible interview questions and your answers. You may need to revise this several times before you get the wording to be as effective as possible. Make sure you are using strong verbs and adjectives to describe yourself. It can help to read your draft aloud and to listen to see if your words sound sincere and convincing.

PEER CONFERENCING/REVISING

When you finish your rough draft, ask another student to look at it. You may even want to read it aloud for the student. After reading or listening, he/she should tell you what he/she liked best about your paper, which parts were difficult to understand or needed more information, and ways in which your work could be improved. Reread your paper considering your critic's comments and make the corrections you think are necessary.

PROOFREADING/EDITING

Do a final proofreading of your paper, double-checking your grammar, spelling, organization, and the clarity of your ideas.

FINAL DRAFT

Follow your teacher's directions for making a final copy of your work.

LESSON NINE

Objectives
1. To confer with students about their writing
2. To have students revise their first writing assignments
3. To become familiar with the vocabulary for Chapters 14-16
4. To preview the study guide questions for Chapters 14-16
5. To read Chapters 14-16

Activity #1

Find a quiet corner of the classroom to hold individual writing conferences. Tell the students to work independently on the other assignments until it is their turn for a conference.

Activity #2

Distribute copies of the vocabulary worksheets and study questions for Chapters 14-16. Tell students to complete them and to read the chapters silently. Also tell them to have answers to the study questions prepared for the next class period.

Activity #3

Allow time for students to work on revising Writing Assignment #1 OR give this as homework assignment and assign a due date.

LESSON TEN

Objectives

    1. To review the main ideas and events in Chapters 14-16
    2. To become familiar with the vocabulary in Chapters 17-19
    3. To preview the study questions for Chapters 17-19
    4. To read Chapters 17-19

Activity #1

    Give each student four 1" x 2" strips of colored paper or index cards–one blue, one yellow, one green, one pink. Have them put a large letter A on the blue paper, B on the yellow, C on the green, and D on the pink. Distribute copies of the Multiple Choice /Quiz Questions for Chapters 14-16. Ask the first question, and have students hold up the colored paper for the correct answer. Then have them mark the correct answer on their worksheets.

Activity #2

    Allow students to work in small groups to complete the study guide questions and vocabulary worksheets for Chapters 17-19.

Activity #3

    Have students assume the roles of the characters and a narrator and read these chapters aloud to the class. Other students should listen & follow along in their books.

LESSON ELEVEN

Objectives
    1. To review the main ideas and events in Chapters 17-19
    2. To become familiar with the vocabulary for Chapters 20-23
    3. To preview the study questions for Chapters 20-23
    4. To read Chapters 20-23
    5. To make predictions

Activity #1
    Discuss the answers to the study questions for Chapters 17-19.

Activity #2
    List the vocabulary words on the board. Ask students to define any with which they are already familiar. Encourage them to identify root words and affixes that may help them understand the meanings. Then have students complete the worksheets.

Activity #3
    Read the study questions for Chapters 20-23 aloud with your students. Encourage them to make predictions about the ending of the story. You may want to have one student record the predictions. After they read the chapters, have students compare the ending with their predictions. Tell them to have the answers to the questions completed for the next class meeting.

Activity #4
    Have students stop reading in Chapter 20 just after The Giver says, "Now for the first time I think there might be a way." Have them predict what the way might be.

Activity #5
    Play some appropriate background instrumental music and read these chapters aloud to students. have them close their eyes and visualize events.

LESSON TWELVE

<u>Objectives</u>
1. To review the main ideas and events in Chapters 20-23
2. To analyze the character traits of Jonas and The Giver

<u>Activity</u>

Explain that an author creates characters, in this case Jonas and The Giver, by giving them traits such as physical attributes, thoughts, beliefs, and feelings. The author develops these traits directly and indirectly. In direct development, the author tells us what the characters' personalities are like. In indirect development, the author lets us hear the characters speak, describes the way the characters look, lets us listen to the characters' inner thoughts, tells us what the characters think and say about each other, and shows what the characters do. Writers sometimes base their characters at least in part on a real person or persons and then elaborate. A good writer will make the characters believable for the readers.

Reread the first two chapters with the students and help them identify one or more of Jonas' traits. Encourage them to explain their answers with support from the text as well as inferences they made while reading. Fill in the information on the Character Trait Chart. Complete the chart as a group or individually. Make another copy of the chart if students will be using it to analyze the traits of The Giver.

CHARACTER TRAITS CHART - *The Giver*

Character's Name _____

Character Trait	Events That Show The Character Trait

LESSON THIRTEEN

Objective
> To practice writing to express a personal opinion

Activity #1
> Bring in an unusual looking object or article of clothing. Ask students to give a physical description of it. Have one student record the descriptive words in a column on the board. Tell students these are facts about the object. Then give your opinion of the article. Ask students to give their opinions and write them in another column on the board. Label the columns FACT and OPINION. Call attention to the words used in the opinion column. Repeat this activity using a sport or a movie or televisions show most of the students have seen. Use pictures or real objects as props.

Activity #2
> Reread the section of Chapter 16 where Jonas and The Giver discuss the feeling of love. Jonas says he understands why the old way was a dangerous way to live, but he liked the light and warmth. The Giver also wonders what would happen if the people had the memories. In the following chapters they decide to give the Community back the memories.
>
> Invite students to discuss the appropriateness of their decision. Then tell students they will have the opportunity to write about their opinion in Writing Assignment #3.

Activity #3
> Discuss the reasons or purposes for writing an opinion paper:
> - to persuade another to take your point of view
> - to inform the readers
> - to explain an issue
> - to help the writer understand his/her own thoughts and feelings

Activity #4
> Distribute copies of Writing Assignment #3. Give students the rest of the class period to work on the assignment. Allow time for students to share their papers, either during this class period or on another day.

WRITING ASSIGNMENT #3 - *The Giver*

PROMPT

Jonas starts to understand The Giver's role in his Community and learns that the rest of the people do not have the memories that The Giver does. He begins to question the wisdom of the way his society is organized. The Giver also wonders what would happen if the people had the memories. Pretend the Committee of Elders is discussing whether or not to give the people the memories. You have been asked to speak to them as a representative of the Community members who share your opinions. Prepare an opinion for or against giving the people the memories.

PRE-WRITING

First, decide on your position: you are in favor of giving the people the memories, or you want to keep things as they are. Make a list of the main points for your position. Decide which points are your strongest and which of the arguments are weaker. List any ideas or examples that will support of explain your points. Decide whether you want to organize your points from weakest to strongest or strongest to weakest.

DRAFTING

Begin with an introductory paragraph that explains the topic and states your opinion. Follow with one paragraph for each of the main points you have to support your argument. Fill in each paragraph with examples and facts which support your main point. Use exact wording and descriptive phrases to help make the Elders understand your position.

PEER CONFERENCING/REVISING

When you finish the rough draft, ask another student to read it. You may want to give the student your notes so he/she can double check and see if you included all of the information. After reading, the student should let you know what was best about your opinion paper, which parts were difficult to understand or needed more information, and ways in which your work could be improved. Reread your work considering your critic's comments and make the revisions you think are necessary.

PROOFREADING/EDITING

Do a final proofreading and editing after you rewrite your paper. Double-check your grammar, spelling, organization, and the clarity of your ideas. You may want to read your paper out loud or tape record it and play it back.

FINAL DRAFT

Follow your teacher's guidelines for completing the final draft of your opinion paper.

LESSON FOURTEEN

Objectives
    1. To complete the plot diagram
    2. To discuss *The Giver* at the interpretive and critical levels

Activity #1
    Work with students to complete the plot diagram. Have students explain their answers with examples from the text.

Activity #2
    Choose the questions from the Extra Writing Assignment/Discussions Questions which seem most appropriate for your students. A class discussion of these questions is most effective if students have been given the opportunity to formulate answers to the questions prior to the discussions. To this end, you may either have all the students answer all the questions, divide the class into groups and assign one or more questions to each group, or assign one question to each student. The option you choose will make a difference in the amount of class time needed for this activity.

Activity #3
    After students have had ample time to answer the questions, begin your class discussions. Be sure students take notes during the discussion so they have information to study for the unit test.

EXTRA WRITING ASSIGNMENTS/DISCUSSION QUESTIONS - *The Giver*

<u>Interpretative</u>

1. What are the main themes in the novel?

2. From what point of view is the story written? How does this affect our understanding of the story?

3. Why was precision of language so important to the Community?

4. Why didn't Lily know what an animal was in Chapter 1? In Chapter 2, why did the author say the bear and the elephant were imaginary creatures? What do you think happened to the animals?

5. What made Father think of calling the newchild by name in Chapter 2?

6. Why did the Community allow the rule about the bicycles to be broken?

7. In Chapter 5, the author says Jonas rarely dreamed. Is this significant?

8. How do you think Jonas felt when he was passed over during the Ceremony of Twelve in Chapter 7?

9. In Chapter 8 the Chief Elder told the Community they could not afford another failure in selecting a new Receiver of the Memory. Why was that?

10. Why was it significant that rules Jonas received said he could lie?

11. Why did the Community release one of the two twins?

12. Why was Gabe able to receive memories from Jonas? What does this suggest about the rest of the Community?

13. In Chapter 16 The Giver gives Jonas a memory of a special day/event. What was described? What do you think happened to the original event?

14. Why don't the people know what happens when someone is released?

15. Why did The Giver think it was important for Jonas to watch the release in Chapter 19?

16. How do you think Jonas felt when he watched the release?

Extra Discussion Questions *The Giver* Page 2

17. In Chapter 21 the author told us that Jonas lied about his day and that his father also lied. Do you think the father really lied? Why would he lie?

18. At the end of Chapter 20 The Giver said he wanted to be with his daughter, Rosemary. What did he intend to do?

19. Was Jonas right to leave the way he did in Chapter 21? Why didn't he try to talk to The Giver first?

20. What items did Jonas take when he left? What was the significance of each item?

21. Why did the Community send searchers for Jonas and Gabe?

Critical
1. Was the story believable? Why or why not?

2. Examine Lois Lowry's use of descriptive language. Discuss some effective examples.

3. Could any of the main events be left out without affecting the story much? If so, which ones? If not, why not?

4. What effect would a different ending have on the story?

5. How would the story change if there were a different narrator?

6. Which character did you learn the most about? Which did you learn the least about?

7. Why didn't the author give the characters last names?

8. Why didn't The Giver have another name? How would the story change if The Giver had another name?

9. The characters spoke in a very formal style. What effect did this have?

10. Discuss the role of color in the novel. What did the author say about the Community in the way the use of color was presented?

11. Discuss instances of irony in the novel. For example, what was ironic about the job title of Nurturer?

Extra Discussion Questions *The Giver* Page 3

12. A euphemism is an indirect or vague way or saying something, a way to give unpleasant things more pleasant names or descriptions. For example, in *The Giver* the word *release* really meant death. It could even have been considered murder. Lois Lowry used several euphemisms in the novel. Find the words and define their real meaning and their meaning in the novel. Discuss the effectiveness of their use in the novel.

13. What was the significance or symbolism of having a baby in the story?

<u>Personal Opinion</u>

1. Did you like the evening ritual of sharing feelings? Why or why not?

2. Why did the Community have the Ceremony in December?

3. Would you like to live in a community like the one in the book? Why or why not?

4. Did you enjoy reading *The Giver*?

5. Is *the Giver* an effective title for the book? What other title would you suggest?

6. If you were to meet Jonas, what advice would you give him?

7. Would you recommend *The Giver* to another student? Why or why not?

8. Will you read more of Lois Lowry's books? Why or why not?

9. Did you have strong feelings while reading this book? If so, what did the author do to cause those feelings? If not, why do you think you didn't?

10. What do you remember most about *The Giver*?

11. What will happen to Jonas and Gabe?

12. What will happen to the Community?

13. In Chapter 23 Jonas felt that the people at the bottom of the hill were waiting for him. What do you think? How could they know he was coming?

14. At the end of the story, Jonas thought he heard music coming from behind him. What do you think he heard?

Extra Discussion Questions *The Giver* Page 4

15. If you could give the Community members one memory, what would it be?

16. How do you think the Community got to be the way it is?

17. What makes Lois Lowry a unique and different author?

18. What questions would you like to ask Lois Lowry?

19. What did *The Giver* make you think about?

20. What picture did Lois Lowry leave in your mind?

21. Did you like the way the story ended? Explain why or why not.

<u>Quotations</u>

1. " NEEDLESS TO SAY, HE WILL BE RELEASED."

2. "I left home at the correct time but when I was riding along near the hatchery the crew was separating some salmon. I guess I just got distraught, watching them."

3. "I'm feeling apprehensive."

4. "Oh, look!" Lily squealed in delight. "Isn't he cute? Look how tiny he is! And he had funny eyes like yours, Jonas!"

5. "I call him Gabe, actually," he said, and grinned.

6. "I think newchildren are so cute," Lily sighed. "I hope I get assigned to be a Birthmother."

7. "Fun doesn't end when you become Twelve."

8. "ATTENTION. THIS IS A REMINDER TO MALE ELEVENS THAT OBJECTS ARE NOT TO BE REMOVED FROM THE RECREATION AREA AND THAT SNACKS ARE TO BE EATEN, NOT HOARDED."

9. "Ash?" he had called. "Does anything seem strange to you? About the apple?"

10. "Larissa," he asked, "what happens when they make the actual release? Where exactly did Roberto go?"

Extra Discussion Questions *The Giver* Page 5

11. "I don't know. I don't think anybody does, except the committee. He just bowed to all of us, and then walked, like they all do, through the special door in the Releasing Room. But you should have seen his look. Pure happiness, I'd call it."

12. "Can you describe the strongest feeling in your dream, son?" Father asked. Jonas thought about it. . . "The *wanting*," he said. " I knew that she wouldn't. And I think I knew she *shouldn't*. But I wanted it so terribly. I could feel the wanting all through me."
"Thank you for your dream, Jonas," Mother said after a moment.

13. "No, no," she said. "It's just the pills. You're ready for the pills, that's all. That's the treatment for Stirrings."

14. "Twenty," he heard her voice clearly. "Pierre."

15. "Jonas has been *selected*."

16. "I think it's true," he told the Chief Elder and the Community. "I don't understand it yet. I don't know what it is. But sometimes I see something. And maybe it's beyond."

17. "Beginning today, this moment, at least to me, you are the Receiver."

18. "It's the memories of the whole world," he said with a sigh., "before you, before me, before the previous Receiver, and generations before him."

19. "You don't know what snow is, do you? . . . Or a sled? Runners?"
"No, sir," Jonas said.
"Downhill? The term means nothing to you?"
"Nothing, sir."

20. "Why don't we have snow, and sleds, and hills?" he asked. "And when did we, in the past? did my parents have sleds when they were young? Did you?"

21. "I have great honor. So will you. But you will find that that is not the same as power."

22. "Call me The Giver," he told Jonas.

23. "How to explain this? Once, back in the time of the memories, everything had a shape and size, the way things still do, but they also had a quality called *color*."

Extra Discussion Questions *The Giver* Page 6

24. "Your father means that you used a very generalized word, so meaningless that it's become almost obsolete," his mother explained carefully.

25. "It's the choosing that's important, isn't it?" The Giver asked him.

26. "It was chaos," he said. "They really suffered for a while. Finally it subsided as the memories were assimilated. But it certainly made them aware of how they need a Receiver to contain that pain. And knowledge."

27. "There could have been love," Jonas whispered.

28. "You know," he said finally, "if they lost you, with all the training you've had now, they'd have all those memories again themselves."

29. "I wish they wouldn't do that," he said quietly almost to himself.

30. "*Do you wish to see this morning's release* . . . I think you should," The Giver told him firmly.

31. "Well, there you are, Jonas. You were wondering about release," he said in a bitter voice.

32. Listen to me, Jonas. They can't help it. *The know nothing.*

33. "My work will be finished," The Giver had replied gently, "when I have healed the Community to change and become whole."

34. "Her name was Rosemary," The Giver said.

35. "It's bye-bye to you, Gabe, in the morning," Father had said, in his sweet, sing-song voice.

36. "It's called snow, Gabe," Jonas whispered. "*Snowflakes*. They fall down from the sky, and they're very beautiful."

LESSON FIFTEEN

<u>Objectives</u>
    1. To extend the story by means of a project
    2. To work cooperatively in a group

<u>Activity</u>
    Allow students to choose one of the following projects. Give them the class period to complete it. If students need more time, you can assign the project as homework or add another day onto the unit.

PROJECT IDEAS

1. Draw a book jacket that summarizes the story.

2. Write a critique of the book.

3. Make a time line showing the important events from the story.

4. Make a diorama showing one of the scenes from the book.

5. Write a poem about the book.

6. Make puppets and write a puppet show to illustrate one scene from the story.

7. Write a radio or television commercial to advertise the book.

8. Design a poster to advertise the book.

9. Write a different ending to the story.

10. Make a comic book version of the story to share with younger readers.

11. Make a mobile showing the main character, secondary characters and setting.

12. Pretend to be a movie producer or director. Assign popular actors to play the roles of the characters in the story. Explain your choices.

13. Create a memory box. Include items that would be significant to the story.

14. Make a collage based on scenes from the book. Use pictures and words cut from magazines.

LESSON SIXTEEN

Objective
>To review all the vocabulary work done in this unit.

VOCABULARY REVIEW ACTIVITIES - *The Giver*

1. Divide your class into two teams and have an old-fashioned spelling or definition bee.

2. Give each of your students (or students in groups of two, three or four) a *The Giver* Vocabulary Word Search Puzzle. The person (group) to find all of the vocabulary words in the puzzle first wins.

3. Give students a *The Giver* Vocabulary Word Search Puzzle without the word list. The person or group to find the most vocabulary words in the puzzle wins.

4. Use a *The Giver* Vocabulary Crossword Puzzle. Put the puzzle onto a transparency on the overhead projector (so everyone can see it), and do the puzzle together as a class.

5. Give students a *The Giver* Vocabulary Matching Worksheet to do.

6. Divide your class into two teams. Use the *Giver* vocabulary words with their letters jumbled as a word list. Student 1 from Team A faces off against Student 1 from Team B. You write the first jumbled word on the board. The first student (1A or 1B) to unscramble the word wins the chance for his/her team to score points. If 1A wins the jumble, go to student 2A and give him/her a definition. He/she must give you the correct spelling of the vocabulary word which fits that definition. If he/she does, Team A scores a point, and you give student 3A a definition for which you expect a correctly spelled matching vocabulary word. Continue giving Team A definitions until some team member makes an incorrect response. An incorrect response sends the game back to the jumbled-word face off, this time with students 2A and 2B. Instead of repeating giving definitions to the first few students of each team, continue with the student after the one who gave the last incorrect response on the team. For example, if Team B wins the jumbled-word face-off, and student 5B gave the last incorrect answer for Team B, you would start this round of definition questions with student 6B, and so on. The team with the most points wins!

7. Have students write a story in which they correctly use as many vocabulary words as possible. Have students read their compositions orally! Post the most original compositions on your bulletin board.

LESSON SEVENTEEN

Objective
    To review the main ideas presented in *The Giver*

Activity #1
    Choose one of the review games/activities included in this guide and spend your class period as outlined there. Some materials for these activities are located in the Unit Resources section of this unit.

Activity #2
    Remind students that the Unit Test will be in the next class meeting. Stress the review of the Study Guides and their class notes as a last-minute, brush-up review for homework.

REVIEW GAMES/ACTIVITIES - *The Giver*

1. Ask the class to make up a unit test for *The Giver*. The test should have 4 sections: matching, true/false, short answer, and essay. Students may use ½ period to make the test and then swap papers and use the other ½ class period to take a test a classmate has devised (open book). You may want to use the unit test included in this guide or take questions from the students' unit tests to formulate your own test.

2. Take ½ period for students to make up true and false questions (including the answers). Collect the papers and divide the class into two teams. Draw a big tic-tac-toe board on the chalk board. Make one team X and one team O. Ask questions to each side, giving each student one turn. If the question is answered correctly, that students' team's letter (X or O) is placed in the box. If the answer is incorrect, no mark is placed in the box. The object is to get three marks in a row like tic-tac-toe. You may want to keep track of the number of games won for each team.

3. Take ½ period for students to make up questions (true/false and short answer). Collect the questions. Divide the class into two teams. You'll alternate asking questions to individual members of teams A & B (like in a spelling bee). The question keeps going from A to B until it is correctly answered, then a new question is asked. A correct answer does not allow the team to get another question. Correct answers are +2 points; incorrect answers are -1 point.

4. Have students pair up and quiz each other from their study guides and class notes.

5. Divide your class into two teams. Use the *Giver* crossword words with their letters jumbled as a word list. Student 1 from Team A faces off against Student 1 from Team B. You write the first jumbled word on the board. The first student (1A or 1B) to unscramble the word wins the chance for his/her team to score points. If 1A wins the jumble, go to student 2A and give him/her a clue. He/she must give you the correct word which matches that clue. If he/she does, Team A scores a point, and you give student 3A a clue for which you expect another correct response. Continue giving Team A clues until some team member makes an incorrect response. An incorrect response sends the game back to the jumbled-word face off, this time with students 2A and 2B. Instead of repeating giving clues to the first few students of each team, continue with the student after the one who gave the last incorrect response on the team. For example, if Team B wins the jumbled-word face-off, and student 5B gave the last incorrect answer for Team B, you would start this round of clue questions with student 6B, and so on. The team with the most points wins!

6. Take on the persona of "The Answer Person." Allow students to ask any question about the book. Answer the questions or tell students where to look in the book to find the answers.

7. Students may enjoy playing charades with events from the story. Select a student to start. Give him/her a card with a scene or event from the story. Allow the players to use their books to find the scene being described. The fist person to guess each charade performs the next one.

Unit Review Activities *The Giver* Page 2

8. Play a categories-type quiz game. (A master follows.) Make an overhead transparency of the categories form. Divide the class into teams of three or four players each. Have each team choose a recorder and a banker. Choose a team to go first. That team will choose a category and point amount. Ask the question to the entire class. (Use the study questions and vocabulary words. For the "Other" category, use more difficult questions from the Extra Discussion Questions.) Give the teams one minute to discuss the answer and write it down. Walk around the room and check the answers. Each team that answers correctly receives the points. (Incorrect answers are not penalized; they just don't received any points.) Cross out that square on the playing board. Play continues until all squares have been used. The winning team is the one with the most points. you can assign bonus points to any square or squares you choose.

9. Have individual students draw scenes from the book. Display the scenes and have the rest of the class look in their books to find the chapter or section that is being depicted. The first student to find the correct scene then displays his/her own picture. When the game is over, collect the pictures and put them in a binder for students to look at during their free time.

CHAPTERS 1-5	CHAPTERS 6-10	CHAPTERS 11-13	CHAPTERS 14-19	CHAPTERS 20-23	OTHER
100	100	100	100	100	200
200	200	200	200	200	400
300	300	300	300	300	500
400	400	400	400	400	600
500	500	500	500	500	800

LESSON EIGHTEEN

Objective
   To test the students' understanding of the main ideas and themes in *The Giver*

Activity #1
   Distribute the unit tests. Go over the instructions in detail and allow the students the entire class period to complete the exam.

NOTES ABOUT THE UNIT TESTS IN THIS UNIT:

   There are 5 different unit tests which follow.
   There are two short answer tests which are based primarily on facts from the novel.
   There is one advanced short answer unit test. It is based on the extra discussion questions and quotations. Use the matching key for short answer unit test 2 to check the matching section of the advanced short answer unit test. There is no key for the short answer questions and quotations. The answers will be based on the discussions you have had during class.
   There are two multiple choice unit tests. Following the two unit tests, you will find an answer sheet on which students should mark their answers. The same answer sheet should be used for both tests; however, students' answers will be different for each test. Following the students' answer sheet for the multiple choice tests you will find your answer keys.
   The short answer tests have a vocabulary section. You should choose 10 of the vocabulary words from this unit, read them orally and have the students write them down. Then, either have students write a definition or use the words in sentences.

Activity #2
   Collect all test papers and assigned books prior to the end of the class period.

LESSON NINETEEN

Objectives
1. To widen the breadth of students' knowledge about the topics discussed or touched upon in *The Giver*
2. To check students' nonfiction reading assignments

Activity

Ask each student to give a brief oral report about the nonfiction work he/she read for the nonfiction assignment. Your criteria for evaluating this report will vary depending on the level of your students. You may wish for students to give a complete report without using notes of any kind or you may want students to read directly from a written report or you may want to do something in between these two extremes. Just make students aware of your criteria in ample time for them to prepare their reports.

Start with one student's report. After that, ask if anyone else in the class has read on a topic related to the first student's report. If no one has, choose another student at random. After each report, be sure to ask if anyone has a report related to the one just completed. That will help keep a continuity during the discussion of the reports.

LESSON TWENTY

Objective

To present finished products for Project Utopia

Activity

Allow time for each group to present its project to the class. Encourage students to ask questions and make positive comments about the presentations.

UNIT TESTS

Short Answer Unit Test 1 - *The Giver*

I. Matching

___ 1. Jonas   A. looked at the Naming List
___ 2. Chief Elder   B. asked for and was given Release
___ 3. Receiver of Memory   C. wanted to have colors and make decisions
___ 4. The Giver   D. the only person who had books
___ 5. Father   E. didn't like hair ribbons
___ 6. Mother   F. had honor but not power
___ 7. Asher   G. had trouble with language
___ 8. Lily   H. received a memory from Jonas
___ 9. Gabriel   I. worked for the Department of Justice
___ 10. Rosemary   J. skipped over Jonas during the Ceremony

II. Short Answer

1. In Chapter 1 Jonas thought about the way he felt. How did he decide he felt? What was causing this feeling?

2. Jonas was chosen, not assigned. For what was he chosen? Why was this important? What was the reaction of the Community?

The Giver Short Answer Unit Test 1 Page 2

3. Describe Jonas's experience of "seeing beyond." What happened? Why was it important?

4. Describe the favorite memory The Giver gave to Jonas. How did Jonas feel about it?

5. What did Jonas and The Giver decide to do for the Community? How did they go about it? Describe the events and outcome in detail.

The Giver Short Answer Unit Test 1 Page 3

III. Quotations: Tell the importance of the following quotations. Include who said each one and to whom that person was talking.

1. "I left home at the correct time but when I was riding along near the hatchery the crew was separating some salmon. I guess I just got distraught, watching them."

2. "Fun doesn't end when you become Twelve."

3. "It was chaos," he said. "They really suffered for a while. Finally it subsided as the memories were assimilated. But it certainly made them aware of how they need a Receiver to contain that pain. And knowledge."

4. "Well, there you are, Jonas. You were wondering about release," he said in a bitter voice.

5. "It's called snow, Gabe," Jonas whispered. "*Snowflakes*. They fall down from the sky, and they're very beautiful."

The Giver Short Answer Unit Test 1 Page 4

IV. Fill in the Blanks

1. Jonas and his family lived in a Community that had gone to _____.

2. No one in the Community could see _____.

3. One day, while Jonas and Asher were playing with an _____, Jonas thought it changed somehow.

4. Later, during the Ceremony of Twelve, Jonas learned that he had been chosen to become the next _____. He realized he was the right person for the Assignment.

5. As Jonas worked with The Giver, he began to want to have _____ all of the time, and to be able to make _____. He and The Giver discussed what would happen if all of the people were able to do this.

6. After a while, Jonas realized he had to go _____. He and The Giver made elaborate escape plans.

7. Before Jonas left, The Giver gave him his most special memory. It was _____.

8. Jonas had to change his plans at the last minute because he found out his father was preparing to _____ Gabriel.

9. The landscape changed as Jonas and Gabe traveled. One of the changes was
_____.

10. Finally, Jonas reached the top of a hill. He found a _____ there and started down.

The Giver Short Answer Unit Test 1 Page 5

V. Vocabulary

Vocabulary Part 1: Listen to the vocabulary words and spell them. After you have spelled all the words, go back and write down the definitions.

1. _____ _____

2. _____ _____

3. _____ _____

4. _____ _____

5. _____ _____

6. _____ _____

7. _____ _____

8. _____ _____

9. _____ _____

10. _____ _____

Vocabulary Part 2: Match the definitions and words.

___ 1. acquisition   A. twisted; disfigured
___ 2. benign   B. violations of laws or rules
___ 3. contorted   C. refreshing; stimulating
___ 4. emphatically   D. miserable
___ 5. invigorating   E. purchase
___ 6. meticulously   F. unrehearsed
___ 7. spontaneously   G. harmless
___ 8. Transgressions   H. alert; watchful
___ 9. vigilant   I. extremely concerned with details
___ 10. wretched   J. expressed forcefully

ANSWER KEY: SHORT ANSWER UNIT TEST 1 - *The Giver*

I. Matching
 1. C
 2. J
 3. F
 4. D
 5. A
 6. I
 7. G
 8. E
 9. H
10. B

II. Short Answer

1. Jonas felt apprehensive. His special Ceremony of Twelve would be coming in December. At this time, he would get his adult job assignment. It marked the end of his childhood and beginning of preparation for adult life.

2. Jonas was selected to become the new Receiver of Memory for the Community. It was unusual because the Community only had one Receiver, and he chose his successor. Receiver was the most important job in the Community. At first he was not sure he was the correct choice, but when he realized he could see beyond, he agreed with the choice. The Community members began chanting his name in approval.

3. Jonas's experience of "seeing beyond" was a short, indescribable change. First it happened with the apple. Next, it happened with the audience at the Auditorium. Then, it happened with Fiona. Her hair changed in a way he could not describe. The Giver explained that Jonas was beginning to see the color red. It was the beginning of his ability to see all colors. The others in the Community could not do this. They gave up that ability when they went to Sameness.

4. There was a tree with lights on it inside a house. Children were unwrapping packages. Jonas perceived *family*. The Giver explained what Grandparents were. He also gave Jonas the word *love*. Jonas liked the memory. He wished his life could be that way, although he thought it might be a little bit dangerous.

5. The Giver said if Jonas escaped and went Elsewhere, the Community would have to take the memories. He knew it would be hard, but he thought it was possible. He would stay with them to help them, but Jonas could never return. He said his job was to help the Community become whole. Then he wanted to be with his daughter, Rosemary.

The meticulous plans they made had to be changed when Jonas learned that Gabe was to be released the next morning. He escaped that night with Gabe.

Jonas took Gabe on his bicycle. They rode all night then rested during the day. Jonas transmitted calming memories to put Gabe to sleep. They traveled that way for several days. Jonas hid them when the search planes flew overhead. He transmitted memories of cold and snow so the heat-seeking devices could not find them. Finally, the planes stopped searching. Then Jonas began riding in the daylight.

The landscape changed as they rode. There were more trees and streams. The forests were thick and dark. They saw their first birds.

After a few days, it began snowing and the ground became hilly. Jonas was forced to leave the bicycle and to walk up the hill. When he reached the top, he was flooded with memories of joy. He found a sled at the top of the hill and used it to slide down the hill. On the way down he heard music and people singing.

III. Quotations
1. Asher had always had difficulty using the correct word. This time, he used the word "distraught" instead of "distracted." The teacher corrected him then explained the meanings to the class. The Community stressed the importance of using precise language, so Asher's errors were considered very serious.

2. Father and Mother were talking to Jonas about the upcoming Ceremony of Twelve. Father was assuring Jonas that he would still have time for his friends.

3. Ten years before Jonas was chosen, the Community had chosen another Receiver of Memory. She asked to be released. When that happened, the memories The Giver had given her were released into the Community.

4. Jonas asked The Giver about Release. The Giver showed him the video of the Release of the twin. Jonas saw his father inject the smaller baby, which killed it. He was shocked. He had no idea that Release meant death.

5. Jonas and Gabe had almost reached the end of their journey when it started snowing. Jonas was explaining the concept to Gabe.

IV. Fill in the Blank
 1. Sameness
 2. colors
 3. apple
 4. Receiver of Memory
 5. colors   decisions
 6. Elsewhere
 7. music
 8. Release
 9. many birds, deer, wild flowers, forests, streams, weather
 10. sled

V. Vocabulary
 1. E
 2. G
 3. A
 4. J
 5. C
 6. I
 7. F
 8. B
 9. H
 10. D

SHORT ANSWER UNIT TEST 2 - *The Giver*

I. Matching

___ 1. Rosemary	A. looked at the Naming List
___ 2. Chief Elder	B. asked for and was given Release
___ 3. Mother	C. wanted to have colors and make decisions
___ 4. The Giver	D. the only person who had books
___ 5. Father	E. didn't like hair ribbons
___ 6. Jonas	F. had honor but not power
___ 7. Gabriel	G. had trouble with language
___ 8. Lily	H. received a memory from Jonas
___ 9. Asher	I. worked for the Department of Justice
___ 10. Receiver of Memory	J. skipped over Jonas during the Ceremony

II. Short Answer

1. What did Father want to do about the newchild, and why? Jonas's father had done something concerning the newchild that fascinated Jonas. What was it?

2. What happened when Jonas's number should have been called at the Ceremony? What did Jonas think? What was Jonas's Assignment? Why was it important and unusual? Did he agree with the committee's decision?

The Giver Short Answer Unit Test 2 Page 2

3. What memories did The Giver transmit to Jonas? What happened to The Giver's memory after he transmitted it to Jonas?

4. Jonas asked why he and The Giver had to hold the memories. What was The Giver's answer?

5. What did Jonas do instead of the original escape plan, and why? Describe the escape.

The Giver Short Answer Unit Test 2 Page 3

III. Quotations Discuss the importance of each of the following quotations. Tell who said each one and to whom they were talking.

1. "Ash?" he had called. "Does anything seem strange to you? About the apple?"

2. "Larissa," he asked, "what happens when they make the actual release? Where exactly did Roberto go?"

3. "Your father means that you used a very generalized word, so meaningless that it's become almost obsolete"

4. "Listen to me, Jonas. They can't help it. *They know nothing.*"

5. "Her name was Rosemary."

The Giver Short Answer Unit Test 2 Page 4

IV. Draw and label a plot diagram for *The Giver*.

The Giver Short Answer Unit Test 2 Page 5

V. Vocabulary

Part 1: Listen to the vocabulary words and spell them. After you have spelled all the words, go back and write down the definitions.

1. _____ _____

2. _____ _____

3. _____ _____

4. _____ _____

5. _____ _____

6. _____ _____

7. _____ _____

8. _____ _____

9. _____ _____

10. _____ _____

Part 2: Matching

___ 1. admonition   A. a reminder of a forgotten task or duty
___ 2. assuage   B. people running away
___ 3. chaos   C. confusion
___ 4. crescendo   D. bewildered
___ 5. dazed   E. very cold
___ 6. ecstatic   F. in an ill-tempered way
___ 7. excruciating   G. agonizing
___ 8. frigid   H. a gradual increase in volume
___ 9. fugitives   I. overjoyed
___ 10. petulantly   J. to relieve

ANSWER KEY: SHORT ANSWER UNIT TEST 2 - *The Giver*

I. Matching
1. B
2. J
3. I
4. F
5. A
6. C
7. H
8. E
9. G
10. D

II. Short Answer

1. He wanted to bring the newchild home with him for extra nurturing. The child was not progressing and would be released if he did not improve. Father thought the extra attention would be helpful. Jonas's father had broken the rule about looking at the year's Naming list.

2. The Chief Elder skipped Jonas's number. Jonas thought he had done something wrong. Jonas was selected to become the new Receiver of Memory for the Community. It was unusual because the Community only had one Receiver, and he chose his successor. Receiver was the most important job in the Community. Jonas agreed with the choice. When he was looking out at the crowd, they changed. He realized he could see beyond and that he was the right one for the Assignment.

3. The first memory Jonas received was the memory of snow. One part of his consciousness knew he was lying on the bed in the Annex room, but another part could experience the sensation of snow and the sled. He could see even though his eyes were closed. He experienced snow, sled, hill, runners, and frigid air. The Giver did not remember it anymore. He had given the memory completely to Jonas.

4. The Giver said the memories gave them wisdom. He explained the request from the Committee of Elders when they wanted to increase the birth rate. The Giver remembered hunger and famine and warfare and told them not to increase the birthrate. Jonas wanted to change the traditional way of doing things and give everyone the memories.

5. Jonas learned that Gabe was to be released. He escaped that night with Gabe. Jonas took Gabe on his bicycle. They rode all night then rested during the day. Jonas transmitted calming memories to put Gabe to sleep. They traveled that way for several days. Jonas hid them when the search planes flew overhead. He transmitted memories of cold and snow so the heat-

seeking devices could not find them. Finally, the planes stopped searching. Then Jonas began riding in the daylight. There were more trees and streams. The forests were thick and dark. They saw their first birds. It began snowing and the ground became hilly. Jonas was forced to leave the bicycle and walk up the hill. When he reached the top, he was flooded with memories of joy. He found a sled at the top of the hill and used it to slide down the hill. On the way down he heard music and people singing.

III. Quotations

1. Jonas and Asher were playing catch with the apple when it seemed to change for a moment. Asher did not notice it. Later, Jonas learned he was beginning to see the color red, and that the other members of the Community could not see colors.

2. Jonas was curious about Release. Larissa did not know what happened to Roberto. She said he looked very happy as he went through the door into the Releasing Room.

3. Jonas had asked his parents if they loved him. They were not sure what he meant. They reprimanded him for using imprecise language.

4. Jonas was upset after he watched the tape of the release. The Giver was trying to help him realize that the people did not really know what was happening.

5. Jonas had earlier learned that the name of the new Receiver who had asked for Release was named Rosemary. Now he learned that Rosemary was also The Giver's daughter.

Vocabulary
1. A
2. J
3. C
4. H
5. D
6. I
7. G
8. E
9. B
10. F

ADVANCED SHORT ANSWER UNIT TEST - *The Giver*

I. Matching

___ 1. Rosemary   A. looked at the Naming List
___ 2. Chief Elder   B. asked for and was given Release
___ 3. Mother   C. wanted to have colors and make decisions
___ 4. The Giver   D. the only person who had books
___ 5. Father   E. didn't like hair ribbons
___ 6. Jonas   F. had honor but not power
___ 7. Gabriel   G. had trouble with language
___ 8. Lily   H. received a memory from Jonas
___ 9. Asher   I. worked for the Department of Justice
___ 10. Receiver of Memory   J. skipped over Jonas during the Ceremony

II. Short Answer

1. Discuss the setting and mood of *The Giver*.

2. Draw a plot diagram for *The Giver*. Label the important parts.

The Giver Advanced Short Answer Unit Test Page 2

3. Discuss the character traits of either Jonas or The Giver. Give specific examples.

4. Discuss the role of color in the novel. What does the author say about this Community in the way the use of color is represented?

5. Discuss the euphemism of "Release" and its importance in the story.

The Giver Advanced Short Answer Unit Test Page 3

III. Quotations Discuss the importance of each of the following quotations from *The Giver*. Tell who said each one and to whom the person was speaking.

1. "NEEDLESS TO SAY, HE WILL BE RELEASED."

2. "I call him Gabe, actually," he said, and grinned.

3. "No, no," she said. "It's just the pills. You're ready for the pills, that's all. That's the treatment for Stirrings."

4. "Beginning today, this moment, at least to me, you are the Receiver."

5. "It's the choosing that's important, isn't it?"

The Giver Advanced Short Answer Unit Test Page 4

IV. Vocabulary

Listen to the words and write them down. After you have written down all of the words, write a paragraph in which you use all of the words. The paragraph must in some way relate to *The Giver*.

1. _____   6. _____

2. _____   7. _____

3. _____   8. _____

4. _____   9. _____

5. _____   10. _____

Write your paragraph below:

MULTIPLE CHOICE UNIT TEST 1 - *The Giver*

I. Matching

___ 1. Jonas   A. looked at the Naming List
___ 2. Chief Elder   B. asked for and was given Release
___ 3. Receiver of Memory   C. wanted to have colors and make decisions
___ 4. The Giver   D. the only person who had books
___ 5. Father   E. didn't like hair ribbons
___ 6. Mother   F. had honor but not power
___ 7. Asher   G. had trouble with language
___ 8. Lily   H. received a memory from Jonas
___ 9. Gabriel   I. worked for the Department of Justice
___ 10. Rosemary   J. skipped over Jonas during the Ceremony

II. Multiple Choice

1. True or False: The Ceremony of Twelve marked the end of elementary school and entry into high school.
    A. True
    B. False

2. What evening ritual did the family perform after dinner?
    A. They went for a walk.
    B. They shared their feelings.
    C. They prayed together.
    D. They did the dishes and cleaned the house.

3. What was unusual about Jonas and the newchild?
    A. They both had pale eyes.
    B. They both had red hair.
    C. They both cried a lot when they were babies.
    D. They both had the same name.

4. True or False: The Chief Elder called Jonas's number then told him to wait for last to get his Assignment.
    A. True
    B. False

Multiple Choice Unit Test 1 *The Giver* Page 2

5. The Chief Elder said the person in the job Jonas would have needed four qualities. Which of the following was NOT one of them?
    A. intelligence
    B. courage
    C. wisdom
    D. agility

6. True or False: in his new Assignment, Jonas would learn to predict the future.
    A. True
    B. False

7. Jonas asked The Giver why the Community did not have colors, etc. What was his reply?
    A. He said a Receiver long before him had lost the memory and now he did not know how to get those things.
    B. He said people had become too weak to know how to deal with those things.
    C. He said that they had disappeared when the communities got Climate Control.
    D. He said another community had stolen them.

8. Jonas wanted to be able to make decisions. What did The Giver say?
    A. He said he thought it was a good idea for Jonas but not for the others.
    B. He agreed.
    C. He said people might make the wrong choices.
    D. He said they shouldn't be allowed to make certain choices.

9. What did Jonas realize as he watched the tape of the Release of the newchild?
    A. The newchild was dead, and his father had killed it.
    B. His father was much more compassionate than he had realized.
    C. His father had broken the law.
    D. His father was a weak and frightened man.

10. What did Jonas hear on the way down the hill at the end of the story?
    A. He heard people calling his and Gabe's names.
    B. He heard laughter.
    C. He heard bells ringing and sirens wailing.
    D. He heard music and people singing.

Multiple Choice Unit Test 1 *The Giver* Page 3

III. Quotations: Identify the speaker by choosing the letter of the correct speaker.

A. Jonas   B. The Giver   C. the loudspeaker   D. Asher
E. Father   F. Mother   G. Lily   H. Chief Elder   I. Larissa

___ 1. "NEEDLESS TO SAY, HE WILL BE RELEASED."

___ 2. "I left home at the correct time but when I was riding along near the hatchery the crew was separating some salmon. I guess I just got distraught, watching them."

___ 3. "I'm feeling apprehensive."

___ 4. "Oh, look! Isn't he cute? Look how tiny he is! And he has funny eyes like yours."

___ 5. "I call him Gabe, actually."

___ 6. "I don't know. I don't think anybody does, except the committee. He just bowed to all of us and then walked, like they all do, through the special door in the Releasing Room. But you should have seen his look. Pure happiness, I'd call it."

___ 7. "No, no. It's just the pills. You're ready for the pills, that's all."

___ 8. "Jonas has been *selected*."

___ 9. "I have great honor. So will you. But you will find that that is not the same as power."

___ 10. "I wish they wouldn't do that."

Multiple Choice Unit Test 1 *The Giver* Page 4

IV. Vocabulary
Part 1: Match the correct definitions to the words.

1. acquisition   A. twisted; disfigured
2. benign   B. violations of laws or rules
3. contorted   C. refreshing; stimulating
4. emphatically   D. miserable
5. invigorating   E. purchase
6. meticulously   F. unrehearsed
7. spontaneously   G. harmless
8. transgressions   H. alert; watchful
9. vigilant   I. extremely concerned with details
10. wretched   J. expressed forcefully

Part 2: Match the correct words to the definitions.

11. stopped progress
    A. permeated
    B. nurtured
    C. efficient
    D. impeded

12. punishment
    A. chastisement
    B. anguish
    C. disposition
    D. aptitude

13. crowd
    A. murky
    B. remorse
    C. throng
    D. crescendo

14. complete agreement
    A. unanimous
    B. conspicuous
    C. conclusion
    D. prohibit

Multiple Choice Unit Test 1 *The Giver* Page 5

15. calm
    A. chaos
    B. serene
    C. obsolete
    D. frigid

16. harmless
    A. precise
    B. torrent
    C. benign
    D. ecstatic

17. fearful; anxious
    A. excruciating
    B. placid
    C. apprehensive
    D. dejected

18. causing to feel energetic
    A. exhilarating
    B. permeating
    C. subtle
    D. efficient

19. noticeable
    A. exquisite
    B. conspicuous
    C. vigilant
    D. invigorating

20. a heavy downpour
    A. optimistic
    B. placid
    C. subtle
    D. torrent

MULTIPLE CHOICE UNIT TEST 2 - *The Giver*

I. Matching

____ 1. Rosemary   A. looked at the Naming List
____ 2. Chief Elder   B. asked for and was given Release
____ 3. Mother   C. wanted to have colors and make decisions
____ 4. The Giver   D. the only person who had books
____ 5. Father   E. didn't like hair ribbons
____ 6. Jonas   F. had honor but not power
____ 7. Gabriel   G. had trouble with language
____ 8. Lily   H. received a memory from Jonas
____ 9. Asher   I. worked for the Department of Justice
____ 10. Receiver of Memory   J. skipped over Jonas during the Ceremony

II. Multiple Choice

1. Jonas was feeling apprehensive. What was causing this feeling?
    A. His special Ceremony of Twelve would be coming in December.
    B. He was failing two subjects in school.
    C. Some other boys were beating him up and he was afraid to tell on them.
    D. He was thinking about a movie he had seen recently.

2. What were the two occasions when release was not punishment?
    A. Release of a newchild and release of a sick person were not punishment.
    B. Release of an orphan and release of the elderly were not punishment.
    C. Release of the elderly and release of a newchild were not punishment.
    D. Voluntary release and release of the mentally incompetent were not punishment.

3. Did Jonas agree or disagree with the committee's choice of his Assignment?
    A. He disagreed with it.
    B. He agreed with it.

4. Which gift symbolized independence and growing up?
    A. The Ones received a name and parents.
    B. The Tens received bicycles.
    C. The Sevens received a jacket that buttoned in the front.
    D. The Twelves had their hair cut.

Multiple Choice Unit Test 2 *The Giver* Page 2

5. From what rules was Jonas exempted?
    A. He was exempted from the rules governing marriage.
    B. He was exempted from rules governing money.
    C. He was exempted from rules governing travel.
    D. He was exempted from rules governing rudeness.

6. What was Jonas prohibited from doing?
    A. He was not allowed to tell his dreams.
    B. He was not allowed to live with his family.
    C. He was not allowed to play with his friends.
    D. He was not allowed to write down any of the memories.

7. What memory did The Giver transmit to explain suffering?
    A. Jonas's wife and children died.
    B. Jonas went back in time to the time before the Sameness.
    C. Jonas walked in the desert without food or water.
    D. Jonas fell off a sled and broke his leg.

8. What was The Giver's favorite memory that he gave to Jonas?
    A. It was *happiness* and *party*.
    B. It was *friendship, marriage*, and *children*.
    C. It was *trust* and *caring*.
    D. It was *family, Grandparents*, and *love*.

9. What did The Giver think Jonas should do?
    A. He thought Jonas should ask for Release.
    B. He thought Jonas should take over as Receiver and then help the people change.
    C. He was too upset to give Jonas any advice.
    D. He thought Jonas should escape and go Elsewhere.

10. What memories did Jonas have as he reached the top of the hill during his escape?
    A. He was flooded with memories of sorrow.
    B. He was flooded with memories of joy.
    C. He understood just how the Sameness had originally happened.
    D. He suddenly remembered Christmas Day.

Multiple Choice Unit Test 2 *The Giver* Page 3

III. Quotations Identify the speaker by matching the letter of the speaker to the quote.

A. Jonas   B. The Giver   C. the loudspeaker   D. Asher
E. Father   F. Mother   G. Lily   H. Chief Elder   I. Larissa

1. "I left home at the correct time but when I was riding along near the hatchery the crew was separating some salmon. I guess I just got distraught, watching them."

2. "I think newchildren are so cute. I hope I get assigned to be a Birthmother."

3. "ATTENTION. THIS IS A REMINDER TO MALE ELEVENS THAT OBJECTS ARE NOT TO BE REMOVED FROM THE RECREATION AREA AND THAT SNACKS ARE TO BE EATEN, NOT HOARDED."

4. "I don't know. I don't think anybody does, except the committee. He just bowed to all of us, and then walked, like they all do, through the special door in the Releasing Room, but you should have seen his look. Pure happiness, I'd call it."

5. "Twenty. Pierre."

6. "I think it's true. I don't understand it yet. I don't know what it is. But sometimes I see something. And maybe it's beyond."

7. "There could be love."

8. *"Do you wish to see this morning's release? . . . I think you should."*

9. "My work will be finished when I have healed the Community to change and become whole."

10. "It's bye-bye to you, Gabe, in the morning."

Multiple Choice Unit Test 2 *The Giver* Page 4

IV. Vocabulary
Part 1: Match the definitions to the words.

1. admonition
2. assuage
3. chaos
4. crescendo
5. dazed
6. ecstatic
7. excruciating
8. frigid
9. fugitives
10. petulantly

A. a reminder of a forgotten task or duty
B. people running away
C. confusion
D. confused; bewildered
E. very cold
F. in an ill-tempered way
G. agonizing
H. a gradual increase in volume
I. overjoyed
J. to relieve

Part 2: Match the words to the definitions.
11. no longer in use
    A. tentative
    B. obsolete
    C. designated
    D. serene

12. ability to learn
    A. disposition
    B. tabulated
    C. acquisition
    D. capacity

13. uncertain; hesitant
    A. remorse
    B. chastisement
    C. tentative
    D. reprieve

14. refreshing; stimulating
    A. invigorating
    B. serene
    C. dazed
    D. excruciating

Multiple Choice Unit Test 2 *The Giver* Page 5

15. overjoyed
    A. contorted
    B. ominous
    C. wretched
    D. ecstatic

16. spread throughout
    A. surged
    B. permeated
    C. subtle
    D. vigilant

17. depressed
    A. efficient
    B. impeded
    C. dejected
    D. obsolete

18. requiring serious thought
    A. capacity
    B. grave
    C. frigid
    D. prohibited

19. violations of laws or rules
    A. chaos
    B. transgressions
    C. rasping
    D. infringed

20. indirect; faint
    A. subtle
    B. primly
    C. murky
    D. dazed

MULTIPLE CHOICE TEST ANSWER SHEET - *The Giver*

I. Matching
1. ___
2. ___
3. ___
4. ___
5. ___
6. ___
7. ___
8. ___
9. ___
10. ___

II. Multiple Choice
1. ___
2. ___
3. ___
4. ___
5. ___
6. ___
7. ___
8. ___
9. ___
10. ___

III. Quotations
1. ___
2. ___
3. ___
4. ___
5. ___
6. ___
7. ___
8. ___
9. ___
10. ___

IV. Vocabulary
1. ___
2. ___
3. ___
4. ___
5. ___
6. ___
7. ___
8. ___
9. ___
10. ___

Part 2
11. ___
12. ___
13. ___
14. ___
15. ___
16. ___
17. ___
18. ___
19. ___
20. ___

ANSWER KEY: MULTIPLE CHOICE UNIT TESTS - *The Giver*

Answers to test 1 are in the left hand column. Answers to test 2 are in the right hand column.

I. Matching	III. Quotations	IV. Vocabulary
1. C B	1. C D	1. E A
2. J J	2. D G	2. G J
3. D I	3. A C	3. A C
4. F F	4. G I	4. J H
5. A A	5. E H	5. C D
6. I C	6. I A	6. I I
7. G H	7. F A	7. F G
8. E E	8. H B	8. B E
9. H G	9. B B	9. H B
10. B D	10. B E	10. D F

II. Multiple Choice		Part 2
1. B A		11. D B
2. B C		12. A D
3. A B		13. C C
4. B C		14. A A
5. D D		15. B D
6. B A		16. C B
7. C D		17. C C
8. C D		18. A B
9. A D		19. B B
10. D B		20. D A

UNIT RESOURCES

BULLETIN BOARD IDEAS - *The Giver*

1. Save one corner of the board for the best of students' writing assignments.

2. Take one of the word search puzzles from the extra activities section and copy it over in a large size on the bulletin board. Write the clue words to find to one side. Invite students prior to and after class to find the words and circle them on the board.

3. Have students find or draw pictures that they think resemble the people in the book. Post them on the board.

4. Invite students to help make an interactive bulletin board quiz. Give each student a half sheet of paper folded in half so it can open. On the outside flap, have each student write a description of one of the characters in the text. On the inside, they will write the name of the character. You can staple or tack these papers to the bulletin board so that the students can read the descriptions and lift the flaps to find the answers. You could also use study questions/answers or vocabulary words and their definitions.

5. Display articles about *The Giver* by Lois Lowry.

6. Have students design postcards depicting scenes from the book.

7. Post articles and/or pictures of different types of communities or societies. Perhaps have students post their own articles and pictures from the introductory activity.

EXTRA ACTIVITIES - *The Giver*

One of the difficulties in teaching a novel is that all students don't read at the same speed. One student who likes to read may take the book home and finish it in a day or two. Sometimes a few students finish the in-class assignments early. The problem, then, is finding suitable extra activities for students.

One thing you can do is to keep a little library in the classroom. For this unit on *The Giver*, you might check out from the school library other books and articles by Lois Lowry. A biography or articles about the author or criticisms of the book would be interesting for some students. Other books in the genre of science fiction would be appropriate as well.

Your students who have difficulty reading or those who speak English as a second language may benefit from listening to the book on tape.

Other things you may keep on hand are puzzles. We have made some relating directly to *The Giver* for you. Feel free to duplicate them for use in your class.

Some students may like to draw. You might devise a contest or allow some extra-credit grade for students who draw characters or scenes from *The Giver*. Note, too, that if the students do not want to keep their drawings you may pick up some extra bulletin board materials this way. If you have a contest and you supply the prize (a CD or something like that perhaps), you could, possibly, make the drawing itself a non-returnable entry fee.

The pages which follow contain games, puzzles and worksheets. The keys, when appropriate, immediately follow the puzzle or worksheet. There are two main groups of activities: one group for the unit; that is, generally relating to the text, and another group of activities related strictly to the vocabulary.

Directions for these games, puzzles and worksheets are self-explanatory. The object here is to provide you with extra materials you may use in any way you choose.

MORE ACTIVITIES - *The Giver*

1. Pick a chapter or scene with a great deal of dialogue and have the students act it out on a stage. (Perhaps you could assign various scenes to different groups of students so more than one scene could be acted and more students could participate.)

2. Use some of the related topics noted earlier as suggestions for an in-class library, as topics for research, reports, written papers, or topics for guest speakers.

3. Help students design and produce a talk show. Choose one of the story incidents as the topic. Students will work in pairs; one student being the host, the other being the interviewee. Students can work together to compose questions for the interviewer to ask. Each pair of students could present their interview to the class.

4. Have students design a book cover (front and back and inside flaps) for *The Giver*.

5. Have students design a bulletin board (ready to be put up; not just sketched) for *The Giver*.

6. Invite students who have read other books by Lois Lowry to present book reports to the class.

7. Invite students who have read a biography about Lois Lowry to tell the class about her life.

8. Have students hold small group discussions related to topics in the book. Assign a recorder and a speaker for each group. Have the speaker from each group make a report to the class.

9. It is not clear what happened to Jonas and Gabe or to the Community. Have students work in small groups to write a sequel telling what happened.

10. Have a read-a-thon during which students get pledges for every fifteen minutes (or however long) they read. Have students come in on a Saturday (or set aside two or three class periods) where students' time can be monitored and officially counted. Use the proceeds for your class's favorite charity or to buy more books for your English Department or library.

WORD SEARCH - The Giver

```
B I R T H M O T H E R B A C K A Y S C S
K F B E W M G F G N I L I A S L K N O T
R T I N L I A R L A V S K S I O R L N E
O C C S A S N L F H B V I L O E R B O E
S T Y R N V E S E R P R Q B V S R B R M
E H C O I Y S W D E A A I I N E L I S N
M B L T M L B S H L R P G E K E T R N G
A A E A A R J M N E M P G A L V L E I I
R S T L R N A T A R L T M W O E V N S S
Y H J U S T I C E S R E D R P L A N E S
T E G C R F N K H E R L P Q A R Q G T A
B R S L R I G L M A O V B M N M A H E G
T E Y A V E T G C Y T S E H Z U G S E N
H Y Y C M J C Y D F Y F R O G I L E N G
R N W O V E M E E M E A N N E V L V U K
E G A M N C N I I C W E A O D A I E R V
E H P M D D H E Y V S L R P C P N T R R
S D I O I C P A S X E R F I M S S U J
H M J P W N T C N S S R L I N U X P R N
T B O K P E G V Z G L T L I O G S A E R
N I N E S O R E B M E C E D E N S I R N
H R A Y C Z P K B B D D N F L J A N C N
T D S R O B E R T O T W E L V E S K P X
```

AGE	CHANGED	JONAS	NINETEEN	ROBERTO
ANIMALS	CHIEF	JUSTICE	NURTURER	ROSEMARY
APPLE	COLORS	LANGUAGE	OLD	SAILING
ASHER	DECEMBER	LARISSA	ONES	SAMENESS
ASSIGNMENTS	EIGHTS	LIE	PAIN	SEVENS
BACK	ELSEWHERE	LILY	PALE	SLED
BEYOND	FEELINGS	LOVE	PILL	SMACK
BICYCLE	FEMALE	MALE	PLANES	TENS
BIRD	FIONA	MATURITY	POWER	THREES
BIRTHMOTHER	GABRIEL	MOTHER	RECEIVER	TWELVES
BOOKS	GIVER	MUSIC	RED	TWINS
CALCULATOR	HIPPO	NAMING	RELEASE	WAR
CARETAKER	HONOR	NINES	RIBBONS	

WORD SEARCH ANSWER KEY - The Giver

AGE	CHANGED	JONAS	NINETEEN	ROBERTO
ANIMALS	CHIEF	JUSTICE	NURTURER	ROSEMARY
APPLE	COLORS	LANGUAGE	OLD	SAILING
ASHER	DECEMBER	LARISSA	ONES	SAMENESS
ASSIGNMENTS	EIGHTS	LIE	PAIN	SEVENS
BACK	ELSEWHERE	LILY	PALE	SLED
BEYOND	FEELINGS	LOVE	PILL	SMACK
BICYCLE	FEMALE	MALE	PLANES	TENS
BIRD	FIONA	MATURITY	POWER	THREES
BIRTHMOTHER	GABRIEL	MOTHER	RECEIVER	TWELVES
BOOKS	GIVER	MUSIC	RED	TWINS
CALCULATOR	HIPPO	NAMING	RELEASE	WAR
CARETAKER	HONOR	NINES	RIBBONS	

CROSSWORD *The Giver*

CROSSWORD CLUES *The Giver*

ACROSS
1. Jackets of Fours, Fives & Sixes buttoned down the __
2. Had trouble with language
7. Had jackets with small buttons and pockets
11. Became the new Receiver of Memory
12. It changed before Jonas's eyes
13. Gabe thought it was a plane
14. Jonas's number
15. Jonas dreamed about her
17. Father broke a rule to look at this list
19. Didn't matter after Ceremony of Twelve
22. Jonas found one at the top of the hill
24. Their jackets buttoned in front
25. Announced the assignments: __ Elder
28. The Receiver had many in his dwelling
29. Jonas, as Receiver, could do this
30. Jonas asked his parents if they felt this for him
32. Wanted to be a birthmother
34. Transferred the memories to Jonas
36. They got names and parents
37. Jonas heard it coming from the bottom of the hill
38. Jonas stopped taking his
40. They had their long hair cut off
41. Jonas's and Gabe's eyes looked this way
42. Father released the smaller of them

DOWN
1. Jonas was able to see __
3. Gabe's comfort object
4. Jonas's Assignment was __ of Memory
5. Adults took a daily pill for these
6. Not an honorable Assignment
8. The newchild who stayed with Jonas
9. The people had never known this
10. The Receiver had this, but no power
12. None existed in Jonas's world
15. These Elevens got new undergarments
16. Month of the Ceremony
18. They got their bicycles
20. The Elders chose these for the Twelves
21. Moving out into the community
23. This wand was a punishment tool for small children
24. This memory made Gabe go to sleep
26. The people could not see them
27. Lily's comfort object
31. Family shared them after dinner
33. Described Roberto's ceremony
25. She was intelligent
37. These Elevens got longer pants with a pocket
39. Jonas recognized when the children played it

CROSSWORD ANSWER KEY *The Giver*

146

MATCHING QUIZ/WORKSHEET 1 - The Giver

___ 1. BIRD   A. Searched for Jonas and Gabe

___ 2. GRANDPARENTS   B. Family shared them after dinner

___ 3. NAMING   C. The Receiver had this, but no power

___ 4. APPLE   D. Jonas liked the memory of them

___ 5. NINES   E. The Receiver had many in his dwelling

___ 6. INDEPENDENCE   F. Jonas's and Gabe's eyes looked this way

___ 7. PALE   G. Fiona's assignment was ___ of the Old

___ 8. STIRRINGS   H. It changed before Jonas's eyes

___ 9. LILY   I. Father broke a rule to look at this list

___ 10. LARISSA   J. They learned language

___ 11. SLED   K. Father released the smaller of them

___ 12. HONOR   L. Jacket buttoned in front

___ 13. ELEPHANT   M. Lily's comfort object

___ 14. CARETAKER   N. They got their bicycles

___ 15. FEELINGS   O. Wanted to be a birthmother

___ 16. PLANES   P. Adults took daily pill for these

___ 17. GIVER   Q. Transferred the memories to Jonas

___ 18. LOVE   R. Jonas was able to see ___

___ 19. BACK   S. What happened to the apple

___ 20. BOOKS   T. Jonas asked his parents if they felt this for him

___ 21. THREES   U. Gabe thought it was a plane

___ 22. CHANGED   V. Had jackets with small buttons and pockets

___ 23. TWINS   W. Described Roberto's ceremony

___ 24. EIGHTS   X. Jonas found one at the top of the hill

___ 25. BEYOND   Y. Jackets of Fours, Fives & Sixes buttoned down the ___

KEY: MATCHING QUIZ/WORKSHEET 1 - The Giver

U - 1.	BIRD	A. Searched for Jonas and Gabe
D - 2.	GRANDPARENTS	B. Family shared them after dinner
I - 3.	NAMING	C. The Receiver had this, but no power
H - 4.	APPLE	D. Jonas liked the memory of them
N - 5.	NINES	E. The Receiver had many in his dwelling
L - 6.	INDEPENDENCE	F. Jonas's and Gabe's eyes looked this way
F - 7.	PALE	G. Fiona's assignment was ___ of the Old
P - 8.	STIRRINGS	H. It changed before Jonas's eyes
O - 9.	LILY	I. Father broke a rule to look at this list
W 10.	LARISSA	J. They learned language
X -11.	SLED	K. Father released the smaller of them
C -12.	HONOR	L. Jacket buttoned in front
M -13.	ELEPHANT	M. Lily's comfort object
G -14.	CARETAKER	N. They got their bicycles
B -15.	FEELINGS	O. Wanted to be a birthmother
A -16.	PLANES	P. Adults took daily pill for these
Q -17.	GIVER	Q. Transferred the memories to Jonas
T -18.	LOVE	R. Jonas was able to see ___
Y -19.	BACK	S. What happened to the apple
E -20.	BOOKS	T. Jonas asked his parents if they felt this for him
J -21.	THREES	U. Gabe thought it was a plane
S -22.	CHANGED	V. Had jackets with small buttons and pockets
K -23.	TWINS	W. Described Roberto's ceremony
V -24.	EIGHTS	X. Jonas found one at the top of the hill
R -25.	BEYOND	Y. Jackets of Fours, Fives & Sixes buttoned down the ___

MATCHING QUIZ/WORKSHEET 2 - The Giver

___ 1. CALCULATOR   A. Jonas liked the memory of them

___ 2. PILL   B. Jonas stopped taking his

___ 3. JONAS   C. Became the new Receiver of Memory

___ 4. LILY   D. Jonas wanted to give them to people

___ 5. ASSIGNMENTS   E. Male Elevens' pants had a pocket for one

___ 6. MEMORIES   F. These Elevens got longer pants with a pocket

___ 7. PALE   G. Jacket buttoned in front

___ 8. BACK   H. Not an honorable Assignment

___ 9. SEVENS   I. Didn't matter after Ceremony of Twelve

___10. MALE   J. Jonas's and Gabe's eyes looked this way

___11. ASHER   K. Had trouble with language

___12. BEYOND   L. What happened to the apple

___13. SAMENESS   M. Wanted to be a birthmother

___14. ROSEMARY   N. Jonas was able to see ___

___15. ONES   O. Jackets of Fours, Fives & Sixes buttoned down the ___

___16. JUSTICE   P. Outside the Community

___17. INDEPENDENCE   Q. Moving out into the community

___18. BIRTHMOTHER   R. The Giver's daughter

___19. AGE   S. Their jackets buttoned in front

___20. GRANDPARENTS   T. The Elders chose these for the Twelves

___21. CHANGED   U. Mother worked in this Department

___22. BICYCLE   V. Had jackets with small buttons and pockets

___23. PLANES   W. Searched for Jonas and Gabe

___24. ELSEWHERE   X. People chose to go to it a long time ago

___25. EIGHTS   Y. They got names and parents

KEY: MATCHING QUIZ/WORKSHEET 2 - The Giver

E - 1.	CALCULATOR	A. Jonas liked the memory of them
B - 2.	PILL	B. Jonas stopped taking his
C - 3.	JONAS	C. Became the new Receiver of Memory
M - 4.	LILY	D. Jonas wanted to give them to people
T - 5.	ASSIGNMENTS	E. Male Elevens' pants had a pocket for one
D - 6.	MEMORIES	F. These Elevens got longer pants with a pocket
J - 7.	PALE	G. Jacket buttoned in front
O - 8.	BACK	H. Not an honorable Assignment
S - 9.	SEVENS	I. Didn't matter after Ceremony of Twelve
F - 10.	MALE	J. Jonas's and Gabe's eyes looked this way
K - 11.	ASHER	K. Had trouble with language
N - 12.	BEYOND	L. What happened to the apple
X - 13.	SAMENESS	M. Wanted to be a birthmother
R - 14.	ROSEMARY	N. Jonas was able to see ___
Y - 15.	ONES	O. Jackets of Fours, Fives & Sixes buttoned down the ___
U - 16.	JUSTICE	P. Outside the Community
G - 17.	INDEPENDENCE	Q. Moving out into the community
H - 18.	BIRTHMOTHER	R. The Giver's daughter
I - 19.	AGE	S. Their jackets buttoned in front
A - 20.	GRANDPARENTS	T. The Elders chose these for the Twelves
L - 21.	CHANGED	U. Mother worked in this Department
Q - 22.	BICYCLE	V. Had jackets with small buttons and pockets
W 23.	PLANES	W. Searched for Jonas and Gabe
P - 24.	ELSEWHERE	X. People chose to go to it a long time ago
V - 25.	EIGHTS	Y. They got names and parents

JUGGLE LETTER REVIEW GAME CLUES - *The Giver*

GEA	AGE	Didn't matter after Ceremony of Twelves
INALASM	ANIMALS	None existed in Jonas's world
PPEAL	APPLE	It changed before Jonas's eyes
RAESH	ASHER	Had trouble with language
SINAENSTSGM	ASSIGNMENTS	The Elders chose these for the Twelves
EONBDY	BEYOND	Jonas was able to see ___.
ICLEBCY	BICYCLE	Symbol of moving out in to the Community.
IRMOBTHHERT	BIRTHMOTHER	Not an honorable Assignment
SOOBK	BOOKS	The Receiver had many in his dwelling
EARRTACKE	CARETAKER	Fiona's Assignment was ___ of the Old
ANDGEHC	CHANGED	What happened to the apple
OLRSCO	COLORS	The people could not see them but Jonas could.
RECDMBEE	DECEMBER	Month in which the Ceremony was held
HSTEIG	EIGHTS	They got jackets with small buttons and pockets
LEPATENH	ELEPHANT	Lily's comfort object
WLSEEHEER	ELSEWHERE	Outside of the Community
NELIFGSE	FEELINGS	Family shared them after dinner
SLEEENV	ELEVENS	Female ___ got new undergarments.
OANIF	FIONA	Jonas dreamed about her.
RABILGE	GABRIEL	The newchild who stayed with Jonas
VEIRG	GIVER	Transferred the memories to Jonas
TRNGPAADERNS	GRANDPARENTS	Jonas liked the memory of them
IPOPH	HIPPO	Gabe's comfort object
ONJSA	JONAS	Became the new Receiver of Memory
USCJTEI	JUSTICE	Mother worked in this department
ANGAELUG	LANGUAGE	It was to be precise.
OLDEV	LOVED	Jonas asked his parents if they ___ him.
OEIMERSM	MEMORIES	Jonas wanted to give them to the people.
OHERMT	MOTHER	She was more intelligent than Father.
SICMU	MUSIC	Jonas heard it from the bottom of the hill.
IENNS	NINES	They got bicycles.
IEENTNEN	NINETEEN	Jonas's number
RRNTUURE	NURTURE	Father's job
IPNA	PAIN	The people had never known this.
AEPL	PALE	Jonas's and Gabe's eyes looked this way.
LAEPSN	PLANES	_____ searched for Jonas and Gabe.
EREIVREC	RECEIVER	Jonas's Assignment was ___ of Memory

Juggle Letter Review Game Clues Continued

EERAESL	RELEASE	Jonas could not ask for this.
OREORBT	ROBERTO	He had a release ceremony in the House of Old.
OSREYAM	ROSEMARY	The Giver's daughter
ISLIGAN	SAILING	This memory made Gabe go to sleep.
ASMSEENS	SAMENESS	People chose to go to it long ago.
ESENVS	SEVENS	They got jackets buttoned in the front.
LSED	SLED	Jonas found one at the top of the hill.
WNOS	SNOW	First memory The Giver gave Jonas
TISRIGNRS	STIRRINGS	Adults took a daily pill for these.
HERTES	THREES	They learned language.
ESLTWEVE	TWELVES	They got their adult Assignments.
ITNSW	TWINS	Father released the smaller of them.

VOCABULARY RESOURCES

VOCABULARY WORD SEARCH - The Giver

```
A D M O N I T I O N A X G V R N X T Q D
A P P A R E N T G F N S F A S T Y H E Z
N D N C D H L E X Q U I S I T E U G A V
E V I E C R E P F C R P U T P R U C P P
Q J Z Y L E V A R G I A O I A U B A H Y
C A P A C I T Y I N Q L M W S G J R A N
D E N H A N C E G Z D P I R O P E T O N
K E C E J P S K I F E A N E B K V S S T
B F S G X C T R D D P B A T S D I O W
E T S I G E E I E B D L N C O J S D P J
N F H E G P M D T I J E U H L V N E T P
I E F R R N L P M U C W H E E S E J I X
G K M I O E A I T K D T L D T D H E M F
N Z E P C N N T W E D E W M E S E C I F
B V H P H I G E E E D Q N T C U R T S W
E K N Q S A E B G D T K A H S B P E T Q
A V H H K V T N M W H L G P T T P D I F
N M U R K Y I I T B U Z M J A L A D C D
G T N E R R O T C B G V R K T E J V Z Y
U P R E C I S E A A T N A L I G I V B T
I P E R M E A T E D L S U C C E S S O R
S P E T U L A N T L Y L R E M O R S E X
H E X H I L A R A T E G Y L M I R P R C
```

ADMONITION	DAZED	EXHILARATE	PERMEATED	SURGED
ANGUISH	DEJECTED	EXQUISITE	PETULANTLY	TABULATED
APPARENT	DESIGNATED	FRIGID	PRECISE	THRONG
APPREHENSIVE	DIMINISH	GRAVELY	PRIMLY	TORRENT
APTITUDE	DISTRAUGHT	IMPEDED	RASPING	UNANIMOUS
ASSUAGE	ECSTATIC	MURKY	REMORSE	VAGUE
BENIGN	EFFICIENT	OBSOLETE	REPRIEVE	VIGILANT
CAPACITY	EMPHATICALLY	OPTIMISTIC	SERENE	WRETCHED
CHAOS	ENHANCE	PALPABLE	SUBTLE	
CRINGED	EXEMPTED	PERCEIVE	SUCCESSOR	

VOCABULARY WORD SEARCH ANSWER KEY - The Giver

```
A D M O N I T I O N A     R       T   D
A P P A R E N T     S   A         H   E
        D     E X Q U I S I T E   U G A V
E V I E C R E P   F   P U   U     R U C
      Z Y L E V A R G I A   I A   R   H
C A P A C I T Y   I N   L M W S   E   A
D E N H A N C E G   P   P I R O   T   O
    E     E     I     E A N E B   V S S
B   S   X   T R D D   B   T S I   I O O
E   T   I   E E I E D L   N C O   S   P
N   F H E G P M D T I   E U H L   N E T
I   E F R R N   P M U       E E   E J I
G   M I O E A I T   D       D T D H E M
N   E P C N N T E D E       E S E C I I
      V   H I G E E D       T C U R   S
  E       S A E   G D   A   S B P E   T
  A       H   T N     L     T L P D   I
  N     M U R K Y I I T     A   A     C
  G     T N E R R O T C B   T   E
  U     P R E C I S E A A T N A L I G I V
  I     P E R M E A T E D L S U C C E S S O R
  S     P E T U L A N T L Y L R E M O R S E
  H     E X H I L A R A T E     Y L M I R P
```

ADMONITION	DAZED	EXHILARATE	PERMEATED	SURGED
ANGUISH	DEJECTED	EXQUISITE	PETULANTLY	TABULATED
APPARENT	DESIGNATED	FRIGID	PRECISE	THRONG
APPREHENSIVE	DIMINISH	GRAVELY	PRIMLY	TORRENT
APTITUDE	DISTRAUGHT	IMPEDED	RASPING	UNANIMOUS
ASSUAGE	ECSTATIC	MURKY	REMORSE	VAGUE
BENIGN	EFFICIENT	OBSOLETE	REPRIEVE	VIGILANT
CAPACITY	EMPHATICALLY	OPTIMISTIC	SERENE	WRETCHED
CHAOS	ENHANCE	PALPABLE	SUBTLE	
CRINGED	EXEMPTED	PERCEIVE	SUCCESSOR	

VOCABULARY CROSSWORD *The Giver*

VOCABULARY CROSSWORD CLUES *The Giver*

ACROSS
1 Twisted; disfigured
7 Very upset; agitated
9 Indefinite
10 Improve
11 Indirect; faint
15 Stunned; bewildered
17 Requiring serious thought
18 In a proper manner
22 Dark; muddy; not clear
24 Crowd
25 Calm
26 Done with a minimum of waste
27 Harmless

DOWN
1 Disorderly confusion
2 Cause to feel energetic
3 Exact
4 Increased suddenly
5 Punishment
6 Distress; suffering
7 Depressed
8 Unrehearsed
12 In complete agreement
13 Violations of laws or rules
14 Extremely concerned with details
15 Decrease
16 Easily perceived; obvious
19 Got in the way of progress
20 Miserable
21 Alert; watchful
23 Heavy downpour

VOCABULARY CROSSWORD ANSWER KEY *The Giver*

159

VOCABULARY WORKSHEET - The Giver

___ 1. SPONTANEOUSLY   A. Regret

___ 2. PLACIDLY   B. Punishment

___ 3. INFRINGED   C. Intruded

___ 4. REMORSE   D. Lovely

___ 5. PERCEIVE   E. Easily perceived; obvious

___ 6. CHAOS   F. Cause to feel energetic

___ 7. TABULATED   G. Disorderly confusion

___ 8. OBSOLETE   H. Refreshing; stimulating

___ 9. DIMINISH   I. Decrease

___10. CHASTISEMENT   J. Become aware of through the senses

___11. INVIGORATING   K. Stunned; bewildered

___12. ECSTATIC   L. Noticeable

___13. ANGUISH   M. Recorded and filed

___14. APPREHENSIVE   N. No longer in use

___15. EXQUISITE   O. Indirect; faint

___16. PERMEATED   P. Fearful; anxious

___17. ACQUISITION   Q. Peacefully

___18. SUBTLE   R. Purchase

___19. DAZED   S. Unrehearsed

___20. METICULOUSLY   T. Threatening

___21. OMINOUS   U. Overjoyed

___22. PALPABLE   V. Distress; suffering

___23. REPRIEVE   W. Extremely concerned with details

___24. CONSPICUOUS   X. Pardon

___25. EXHILARATE   Y. Spread or flowing throughout

KEY: VOCABULARY WORKSHEET - The Giver

S - 1. SPONTANEOUSLY   A. Regret
Q - 2. PLACIDLY   B. Punishment
C - 3. INFRINGED   C. Intruded
A - 4. REMORSE   D. Lovely
J - 5. PERCEIVE   E. Easily perceived; obvious
G - 6. CHAOS   F. Cause to feel energetic
M - 7. TABULATED   G. Disorderly confusion
N - 8. OBSOLETE   H. Refreshing; stimulating
I - 9. DIMINISH   I. Decrease
B -10. CHASTISEMENT   J. Become aware of through the senses
H -11. INVIGORATING   K. Stunned; bewildered
U -12. ECSTATIC   L. Noticeable
V -13. ANGUISH   M. Recorded and filed
P -14. APPREHENSIVE   N. No longer in use
D -15. EXQUISITE   O. Indirect; faint
Y -16. PERMEATED   P. Fearful; anxious
R -17. ACQUISITION   Q. Peacefully
O -18. SUBTLE   R. Purchase
K -19. DAZED   S. Unrehearsed
W 20. METICULOUSLY   T. Threatening
T -21. OMINOUS   U. Overjoyed
E -22. PALPABLE   V. Distress; suffering
X -23. REPRIEVE   W. Extremely concerned with details
L -24. CONSPICUOUS   X. Pardon
F -25. EXHILARATE   Y. Spread or flowing throughout

VOCABULARY MULTIPLE CHOICE - The Giver

____ 1. Recorded and filed
   A. SUCCESSOR B. PALPABLE C. TABULATED D. DAZED

____ 2. Fearful; anxious
   A. CONCLUSION B. TENTATIVELY C. APPREHENSIVE D. CONSPICUOUS

____ 3. One who comes next
   A. IMPEDED B. METICULOUSLY C. SUCCESSOR D. PRIMLY

____ 4. Calm
   A. ASSUAGE B. CAPACITY C. SERENE D. EXCRUCIATING

____ 5. Twisted; disfigured
   A. CONTORTED B. THRONG C. WRETCHED D. CAPACITY

____ 6. Very upset; agitated
   A. PERMEATED B. DISTRAUGHT C. FUGITIVES D. ASSUAGE

____ 7. Talent
   A. APTITUDE B. SERENE C. CONTORTED D. PERMEATED

____ 8. Become aware of through the senses
   A. VIGILANT B. FUGITIVES C. ENHANCE D. PERCEIVE

____ 9. People running away
   A. FUGITIVES B. ECSTATIC C. TRANSGRESSIONS D. WRETCHED

____ 10. Unrehearsed
   A. CONTORTED B. SPONTANEOUSLY C. CRESCENDO D. CHASTISEMENT

____ 11. Very cold
   A. DISPOSITION B. SURGED C. CRESCENDO D. FRIGID

____ 12. Forbidden
   A. PROHIBITED B. METICULOUSLY C. CHAOS D. SPONTANEOUSLY

____ 13. To relieve
   A. DAZED B. ASSUAGE C. TABULATED D. DISTRAUGHT

____ 14. Overjoyed
   A. SUCCESSOR B. ECSTATIC C. EXQUISITE D. GRAVELY

____ 15. Regret
   A. OPTIMISTIC B. APTITUDE C. REMORSE D. OBSOLETE

____ 16. Agonizing
   A. APPREHENSIVE B. TABULATED C. DESIGNATED D. EXCRUCIATING

____ 17. Threatening
   A. VAGUE B. APTITUDE C. FUGITIVES D. OMINOUS

____ 18. Hopeful; expecting the best outcome
   A. THRONG B. BENIGN C. OPTIMISTIC D. EXCRUCIATING

____19. Indefinite
   A. RASPING B. VAGUE C. INVIGORATING D. WRETCHED

____20. Indicated; pointed out
   A. APPARENT B. DESIGNATED C. EXQUISITE D. VIGILANT

____21. Dark; muddy; not clear
   A. RASPING B. APPARENT C. PRIMLY D. MURKY

____22. Helping to grow or develop
   A. TRANSGRESSIONS B. SERENE C. VAGUE D. NURTURING

____23. Distress; suffering
   A. MURKY B. TABULATED C. THRONG D. ANGUISH

____24. Spread or flowing throughout
   A. CHASTISEMENT B. VIGILANT C. PERMEATED D. CRINGED

____25. Gradual increase in volume
   A. FUGITIVES B. EXHILARATE C. CRESCENDO D. EXUBERANT

KEY: VOCABULARY MULTIPLE CHOICE - The Giver

C-> 1. Recorded and filed
  A. SUCCESSOR B. PALPABLE C. TABULATED D. DAZED

C-> 2. Fearful; anxious
  A. CONCLUSION B. TENTATIVELY C. APPREHENSIVE D. CONSPICUOUS

C-> 3. One who comes next
  A. IMPEDED B. METICULOUSLY C. SUCCESSOR D. PRIMLY

C-> 4. Calm
  A. ASSUAGE B. CAPACITY C. SERENE D. EXCRUCIATING

A-> 5. Twisted; disfigured
  A. CONTORTED B. THRONG C. WRETCHED D. CAPACITY

B-> 6. Very upset; agitated
  A. PERMEATED B. DISTRAUGHT C. FUGITIVES D. ASSUAGE

A-> 7. Talent
  A. APTITUDE B. SERENE C. CONTORTED D. PERMEATED

D-> 8. Become aware of through the senses
  A. VIGILANT B. FUGITIVES C. ENHANCE D. PERCEIVE

A-> 9. People running away
  A. FUGITIVES B. ECSTATIC C. TRANSGRESSIONS D. WRETCHED

B-> 10. Unrehearsed
  A. CONTORTED B. SPONTANEOUSLY C. CRESCENDO D. CHASTISEMENT

D-> 11. Very cold
  A. DISPOSITION B. SURGED C. CRESCENDO D. FRIGID

A-> 12. Forbidden
  A. PROHIBITED B. METICULOUSLY C. CHAOS D. SPONTANEOUSLY

B-> 13. To relieve
  A. DAZED B. ASSUAGE C. TABULATED D. DISTRAUGHT

B-> 14. Overjoyed
  A. SUCCESSOR B. ECSTATIC C. EXQUISITE D. GRAVELY

C-> 15. Regret
  A. OPTIMISTIC B. APTITUDE C. REMORSE D. OBSOLETE

D-> 16. Agonizing
  A. APPREHENSIVE B. TABULATED C. DESIGNATED D. EXCRUCIATING

D-> 17. Threatening
  A. VAGUE B. APTITUDE C. FUGITIVES D. OMINOUS

C-> 18. Hopeful; expecting the best outcome
  A. THRONG B. BENIGN C. OPTIMISTIC D. EXCRUCIATING

B-> 19. Indefinite
   A. RASPING B. VAGUE C. INVIGORATING D. WRETCHED

B-> 20. Indicated; pointed out
   A. APPARENT B. DESIGNATED C. EXQUISITE D. VIGILANT

D-> 21. Dark; muddy; not clear
   A. RASPING B. APPARENT C. PRIMLY D. MURKY

D-> 22. Helping to grow or develop
   A. TRANSGRESSIONS B. SERENE C. VAGUE D. NURTURING

D-> 23. Distress; suffering
   A. MURKY B. TABULATED C. THRONG D. ANGUISH

C-> 24. Spread or flowing throughout
   A. CHASTISEMENT B. VIGILANT C. PERMEATED D. CRINGED

C-> 25. Gradual increase in volume
   A. FUGITIVES B. EXHILARATE C. CRESCENDO D. EXUBERANT

VOCABULARY JUGGLE LETTER REVIEW GAME CLUES - *The Giver*

ICQOUDAITNI	ACQUISITION	Purchase
AOMODNIINT	ADMONITION	A reminder of a forgotten task or duty
UNISHAG	ANGUISH	Distress; suffering
RPPANEAT	APPARENT	Visible; easily seen
TDIATEUP	APTITUDE	Talent
SAUSAGE	ASSUAGE	To relieve
GENINB	BENIGN	Harmless
YAACICPT	CAPACITY	Ability to learn
HASCO	CHAOS	Confusion
ODTORCTEN	CONTORTED	Twisted; disfigured
RSECDEOCN	CRESCENDO	A gradual increase in volume
INERDGC	CRINGED	Shrank back in fear
AEDDZ	DAZED	Confused; bewildered
EJETEDDC	DEJECTED	Depressed
MIINIHDS	DIMINISH	Decrease
ACTECTIS	ECSTATIC	Overjoyed
CFFIEITNE	EFFICIENT	Done with a minimum of waste
HAECENN	ENHANCE	Improve
DEEPXTEM	EXEMPTED	Freed from obligation
DRIFGI	FRIGID	Very cold
ITIFUVESG	FUGITIVES	People running away
AELRGYV	GRAVELY	Requiring serious thought
PEDIEMD	IMPEDED	Stopped in progress
GNFDRINIE	INFRINGED	Intruded
YRKMU	MURKY	Dark
RTUGRNINU	NURTURING	Helping to grow or develop
BOLEEOSST	OBSOLETE	No longer in use
SMOINUO	OMINOUS	Unfavorable; threatening
TPITIIOCSM	OPTIMISTIC	Hopeful; expecting the best
PELPAALB	PALPABLE	Easily perceived; obvious
VECPEIRE	PERCEIVE	To become aware of through the senses
LACPIDYL	PLACIDLY	Peacefully
RECIPES	PRECISE	Exact
HROPIITEDB	PROHIBITED	Forbidden
AGSPRIN	RASPING	A harsh, grating sound
MORSERE	REMORSE	Regret
EPIERVER	REPRIEVE	Pardon
RSEEEN	SERENE	Calm
BUSTLE	SUBTLE	Indirect; faint